mates &
Blokes

Peter Slater

FOR ALL MY

mates

mate1

/meɪt/

noun

suffix: -mates; plural noun: mates

1.

the sexual partner of a bird or other animal.

"a male bird sings to court a mate"

2.

a fellow member or joint occupant of a specified thing.

"his table-mates"

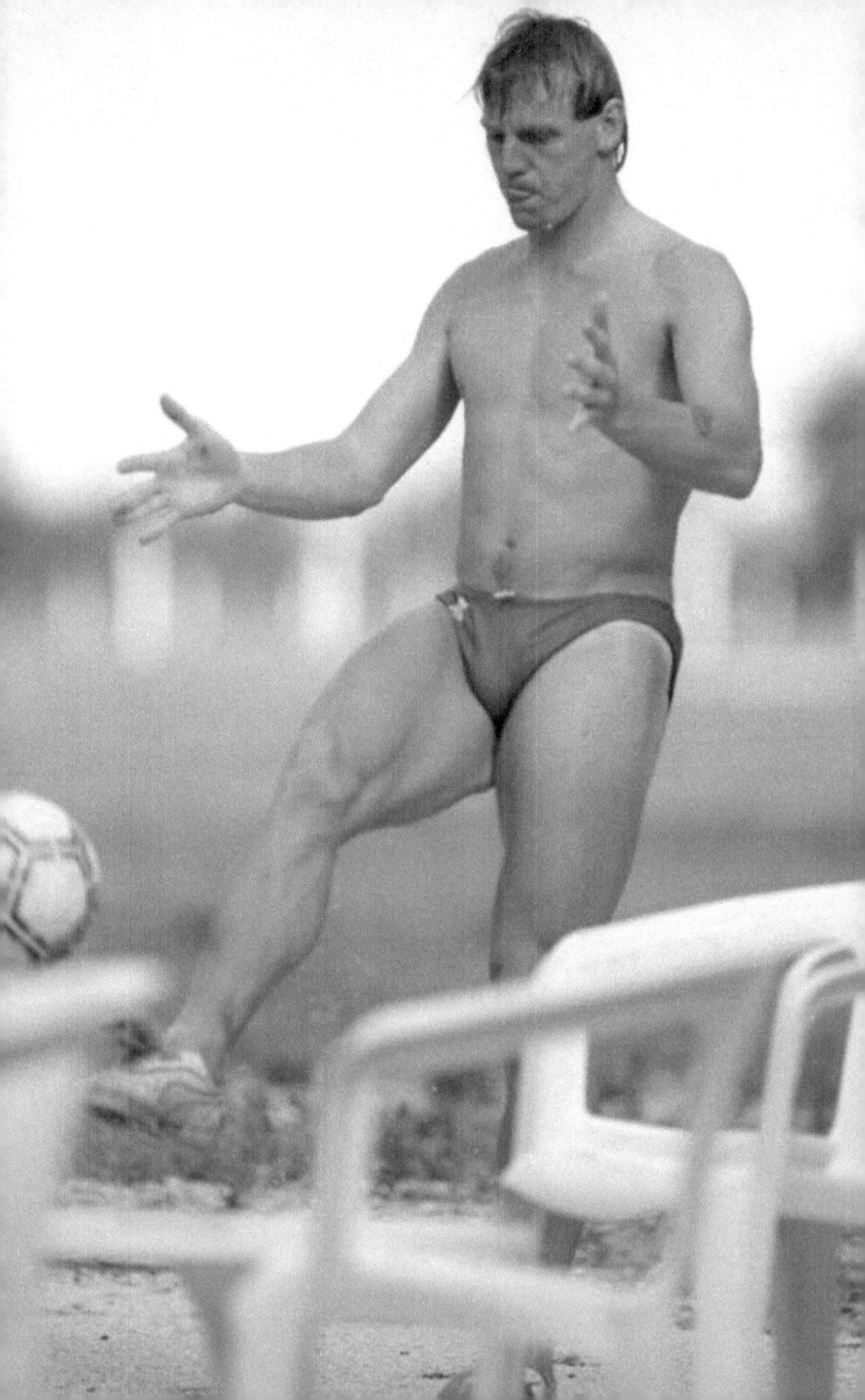

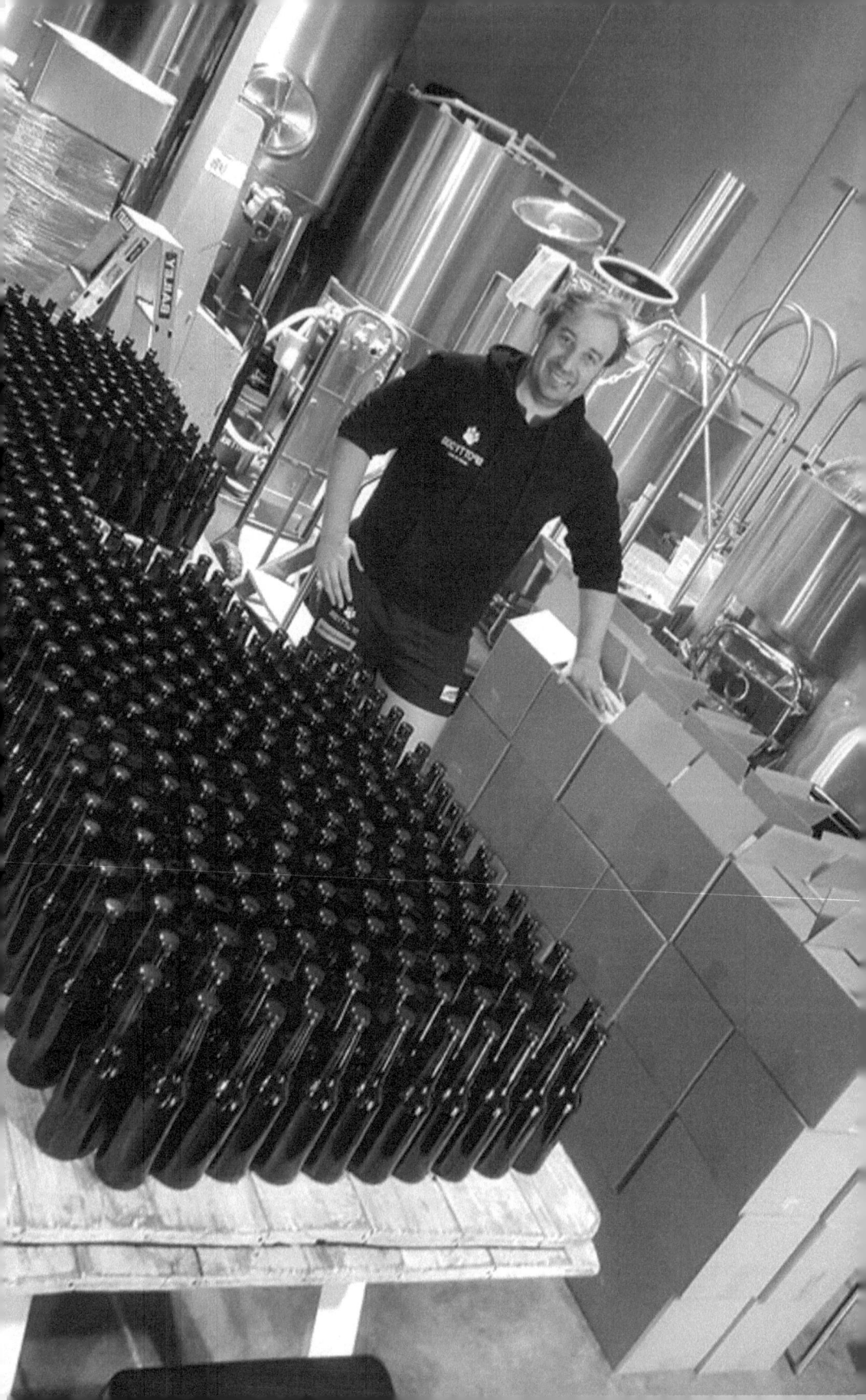

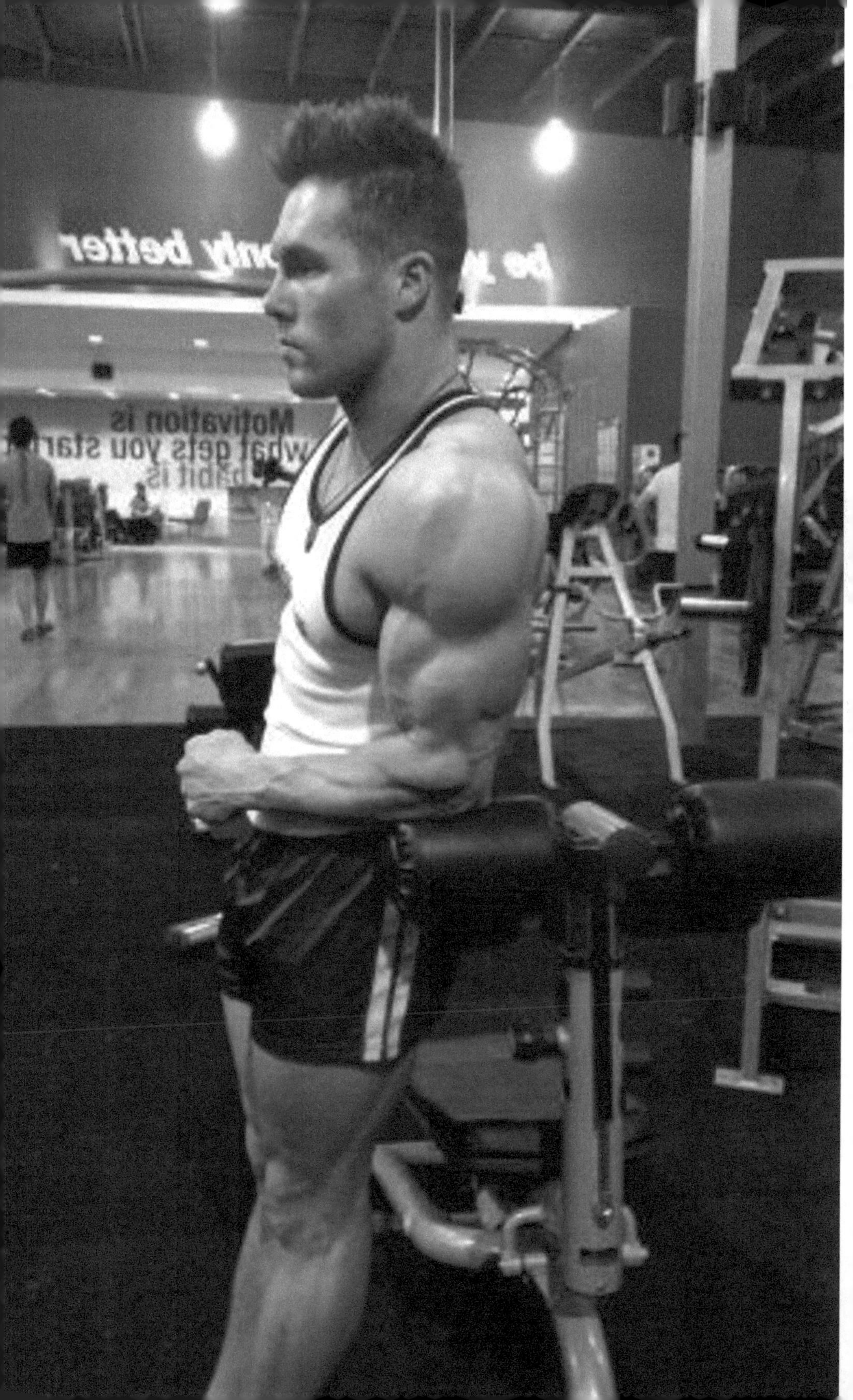
Motivation is

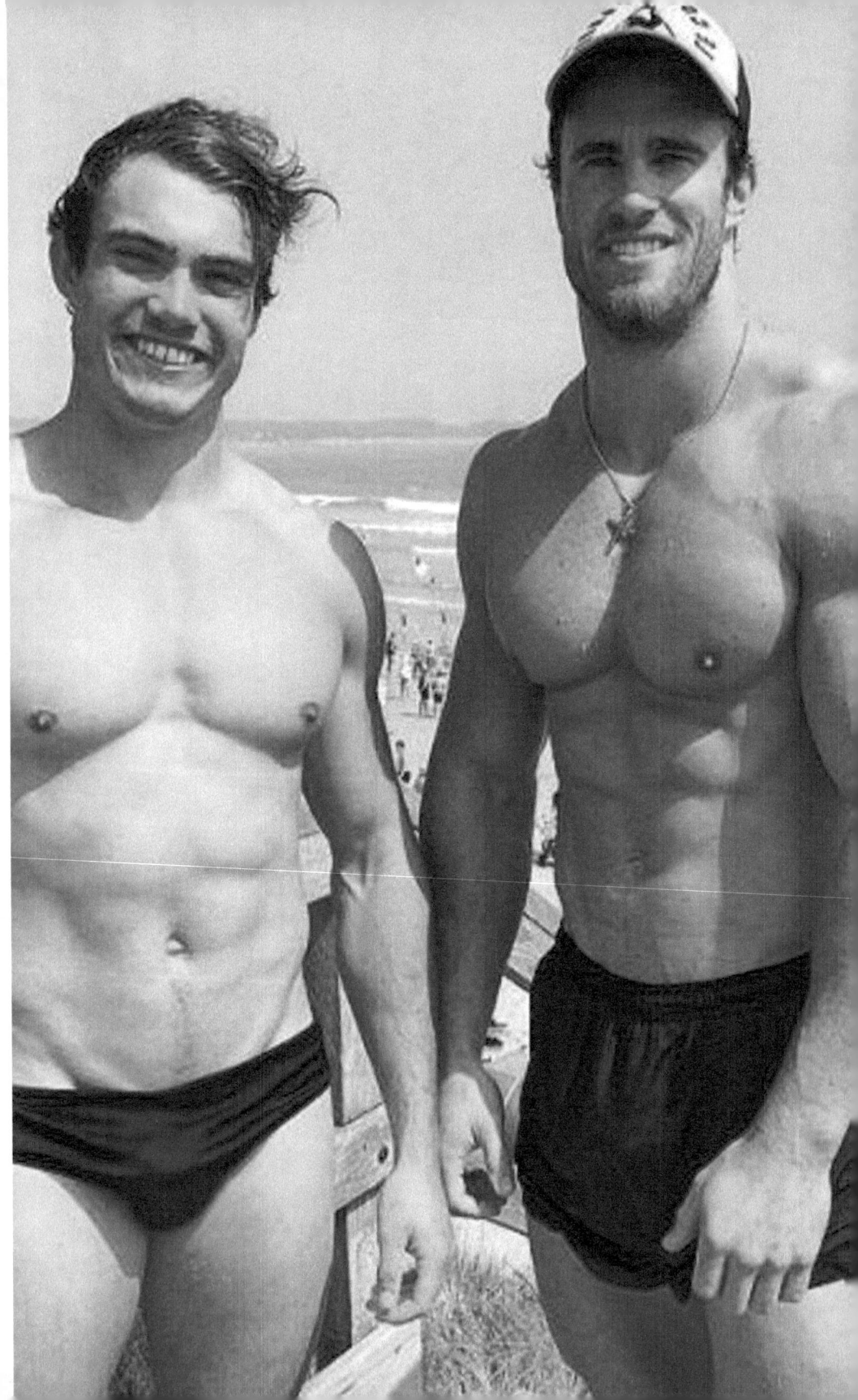

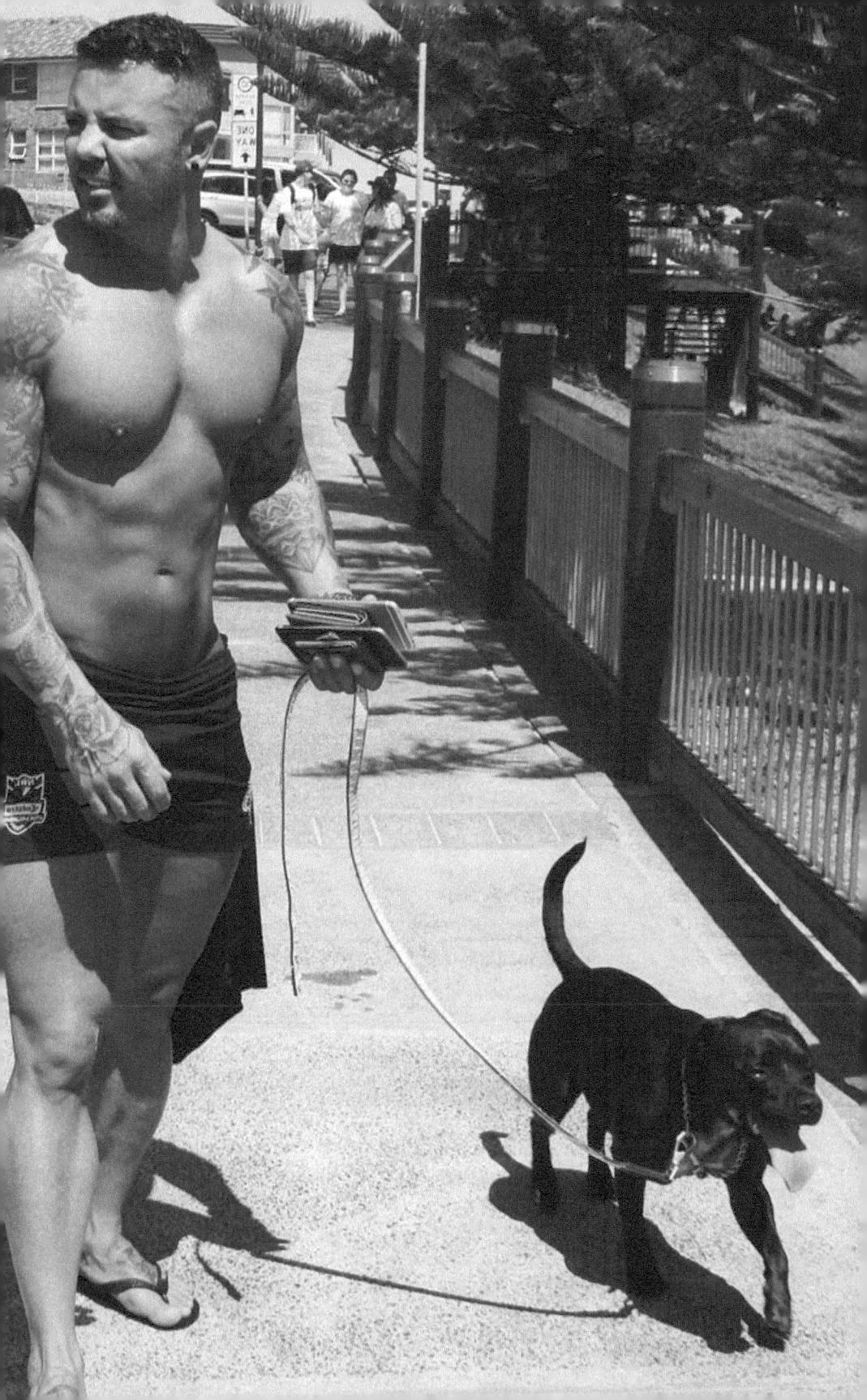

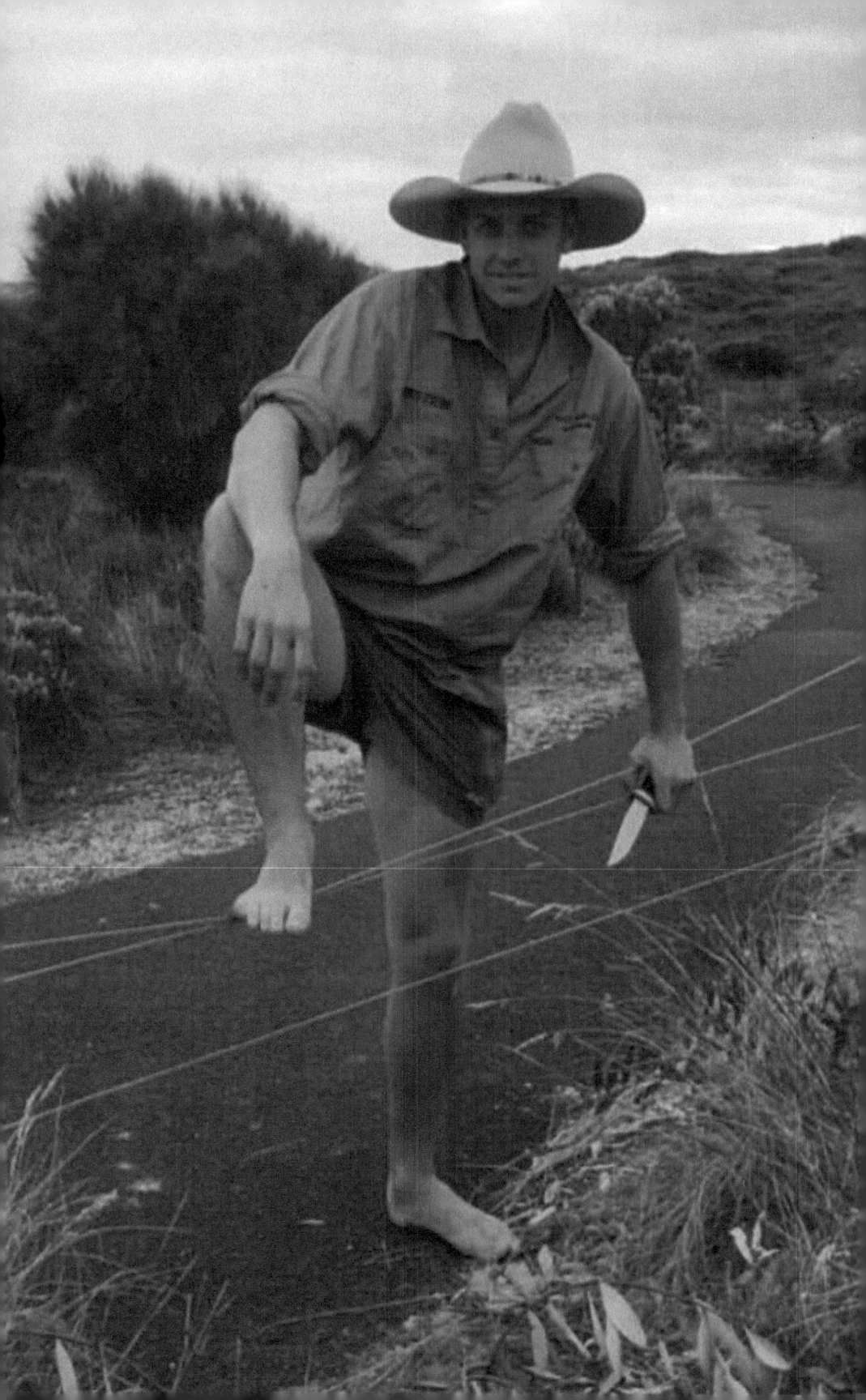

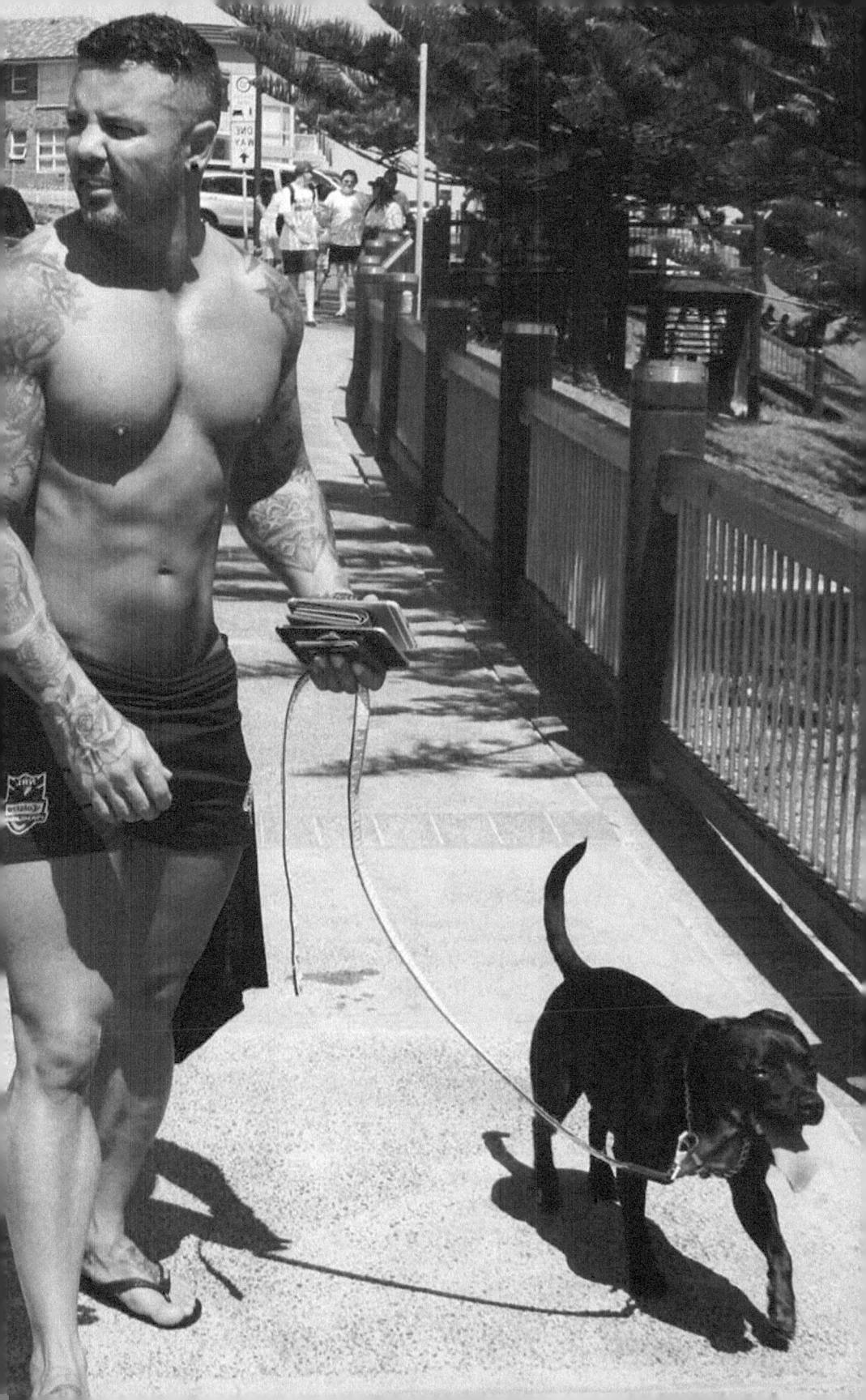

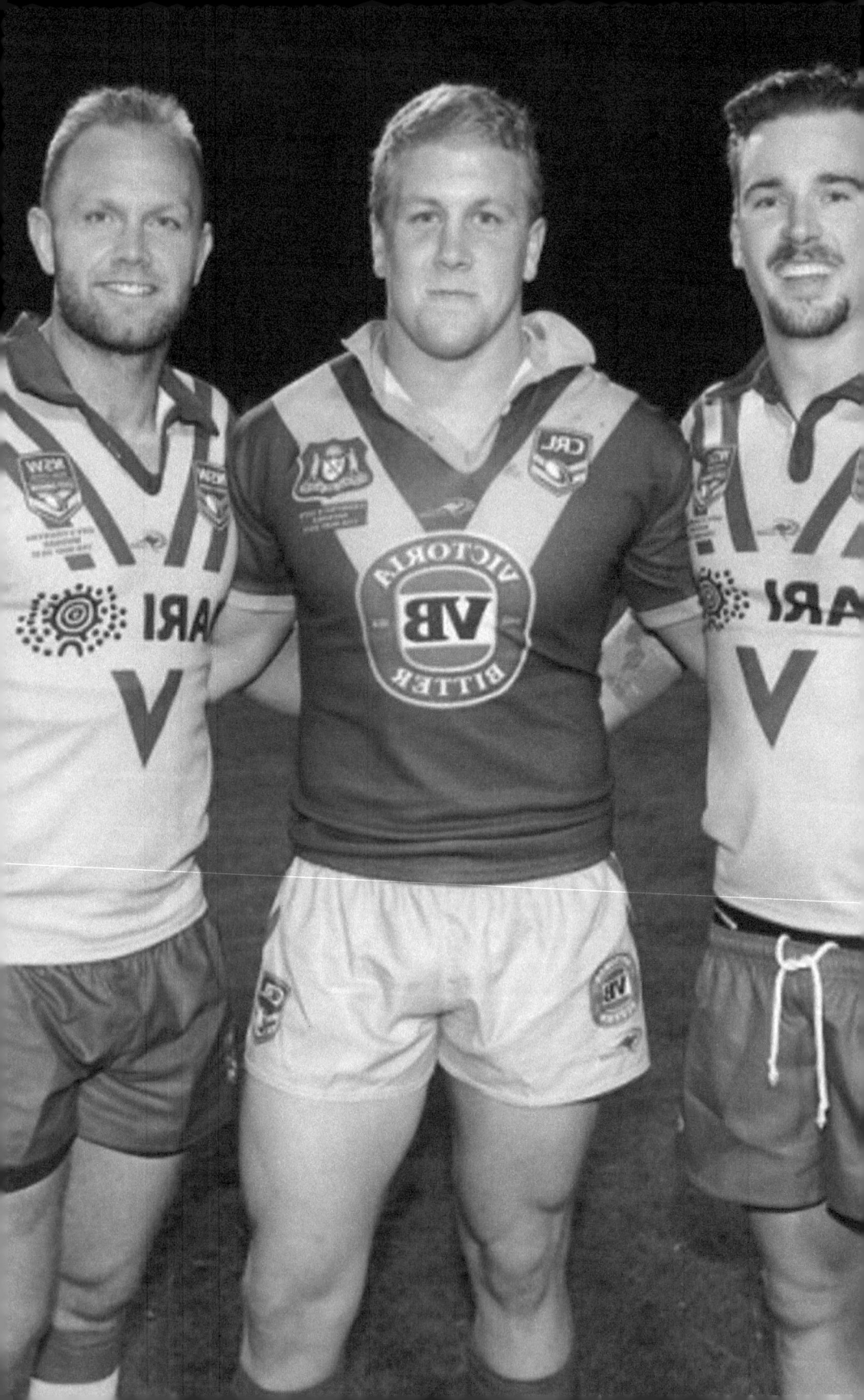

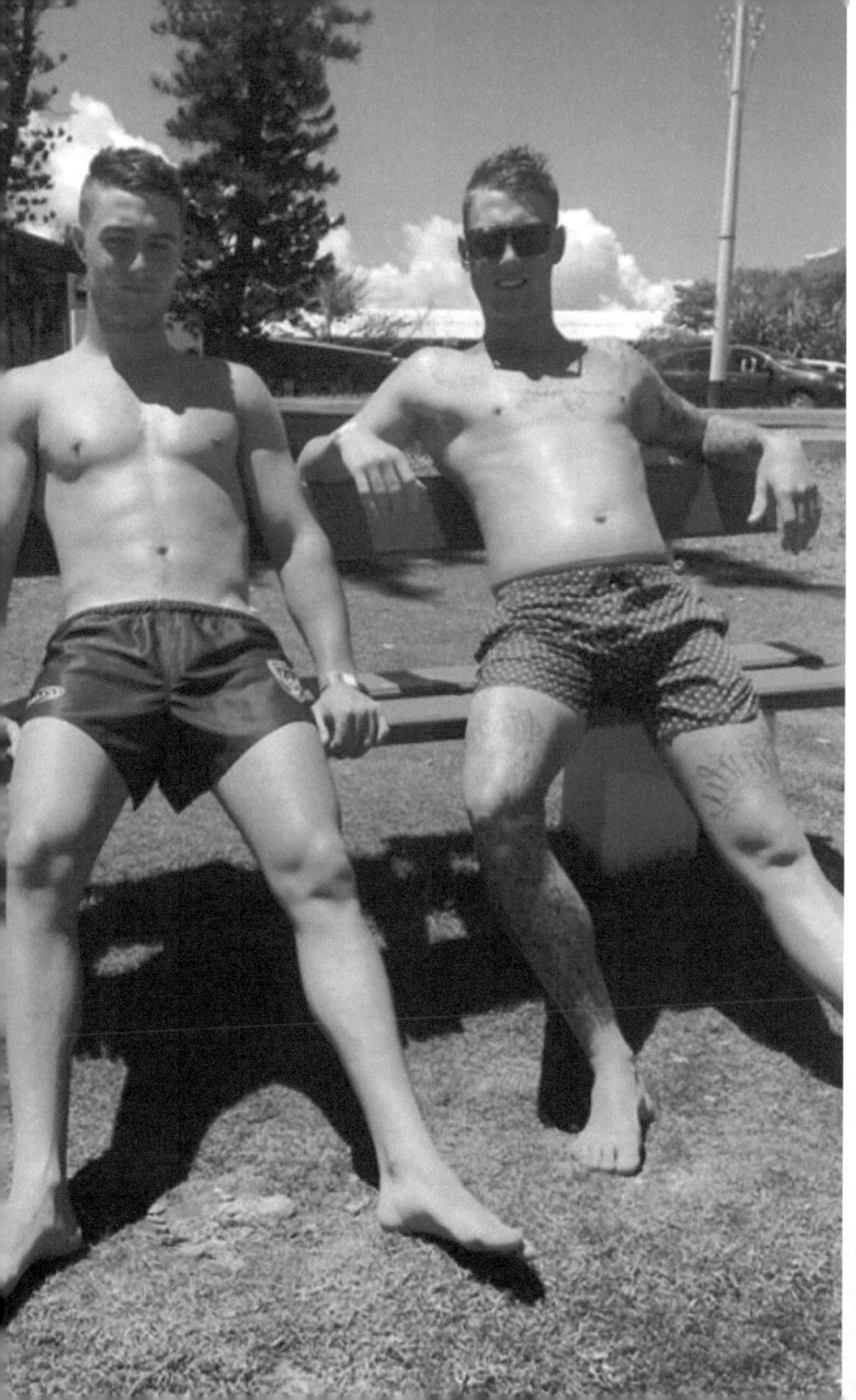

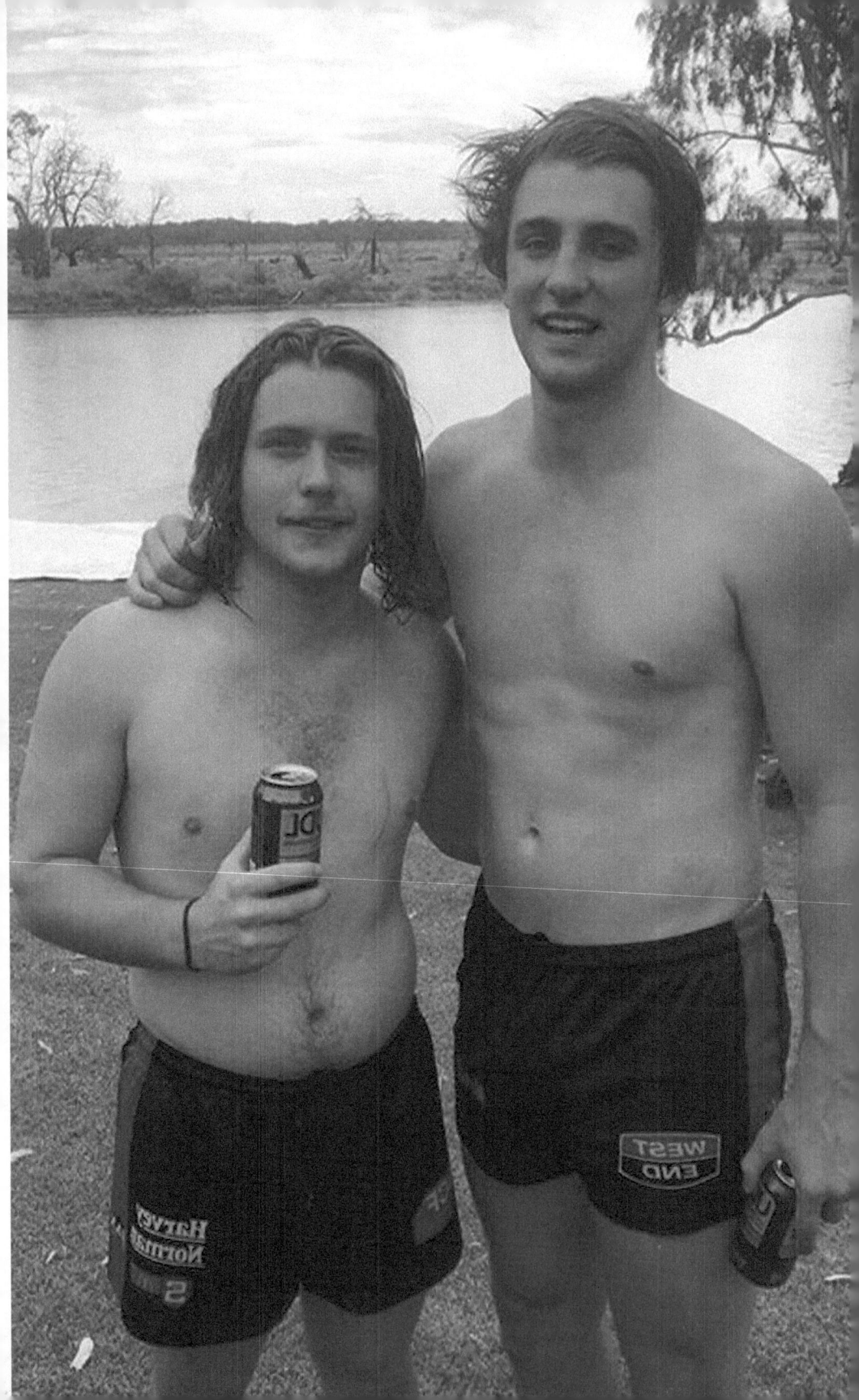

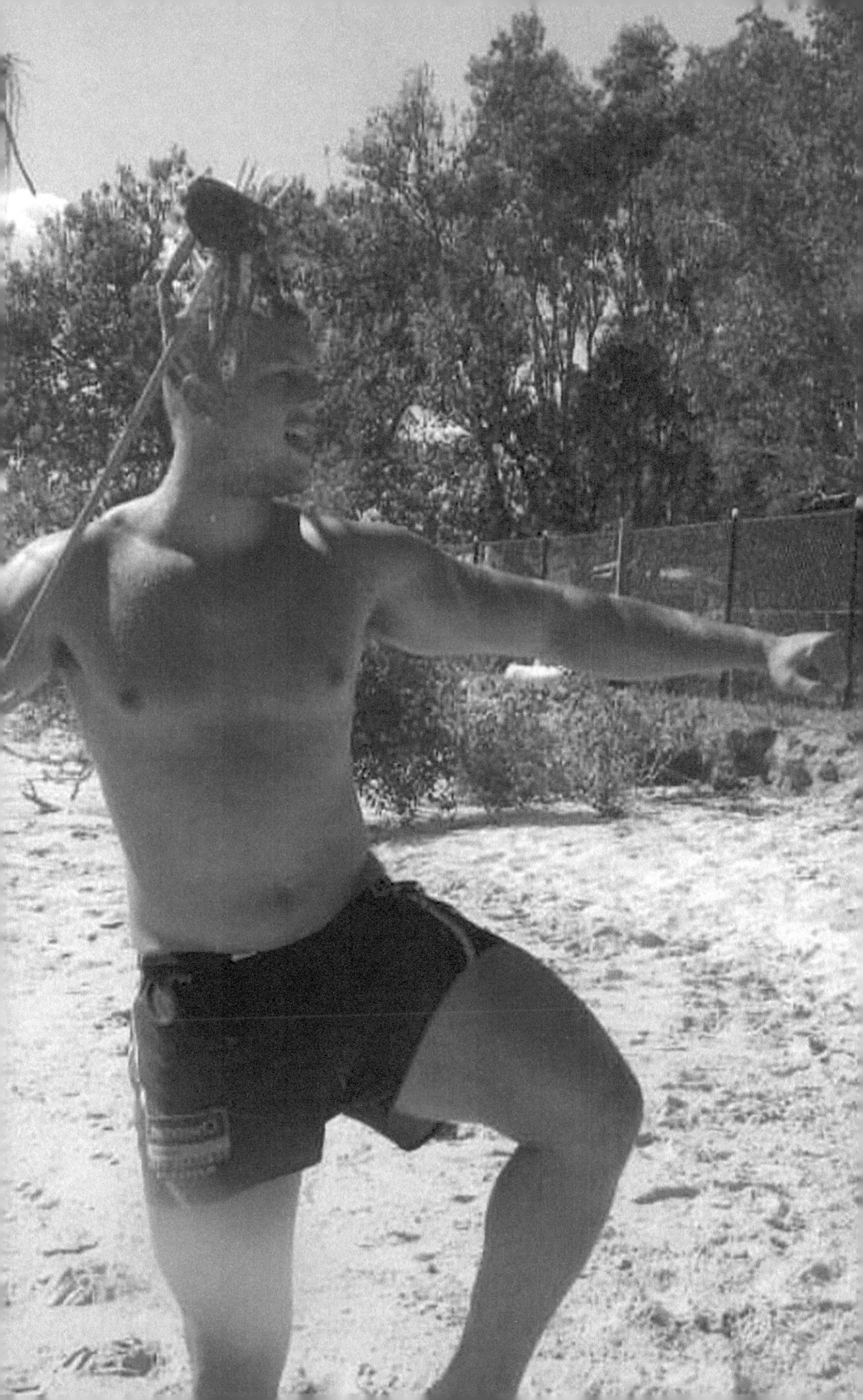

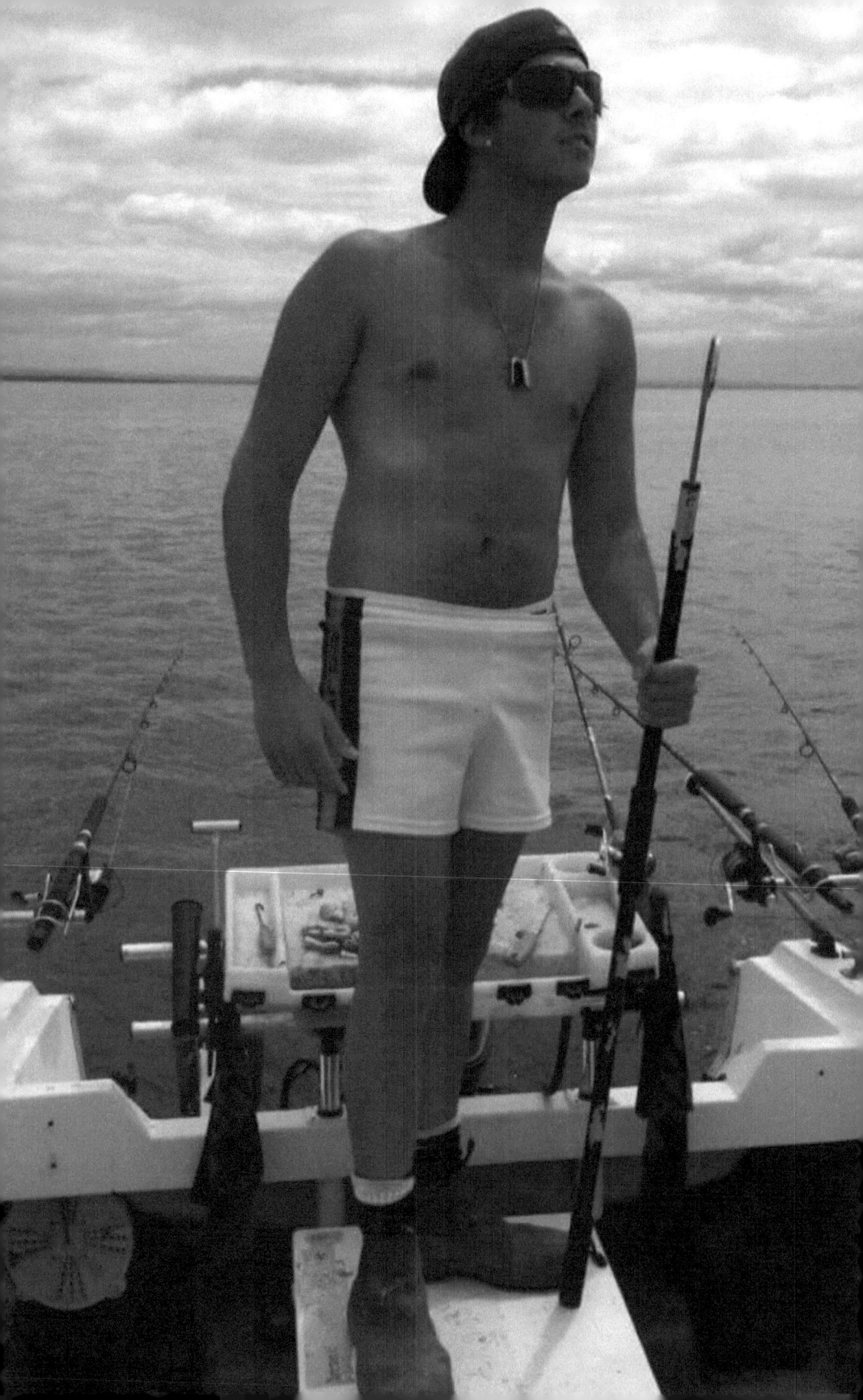

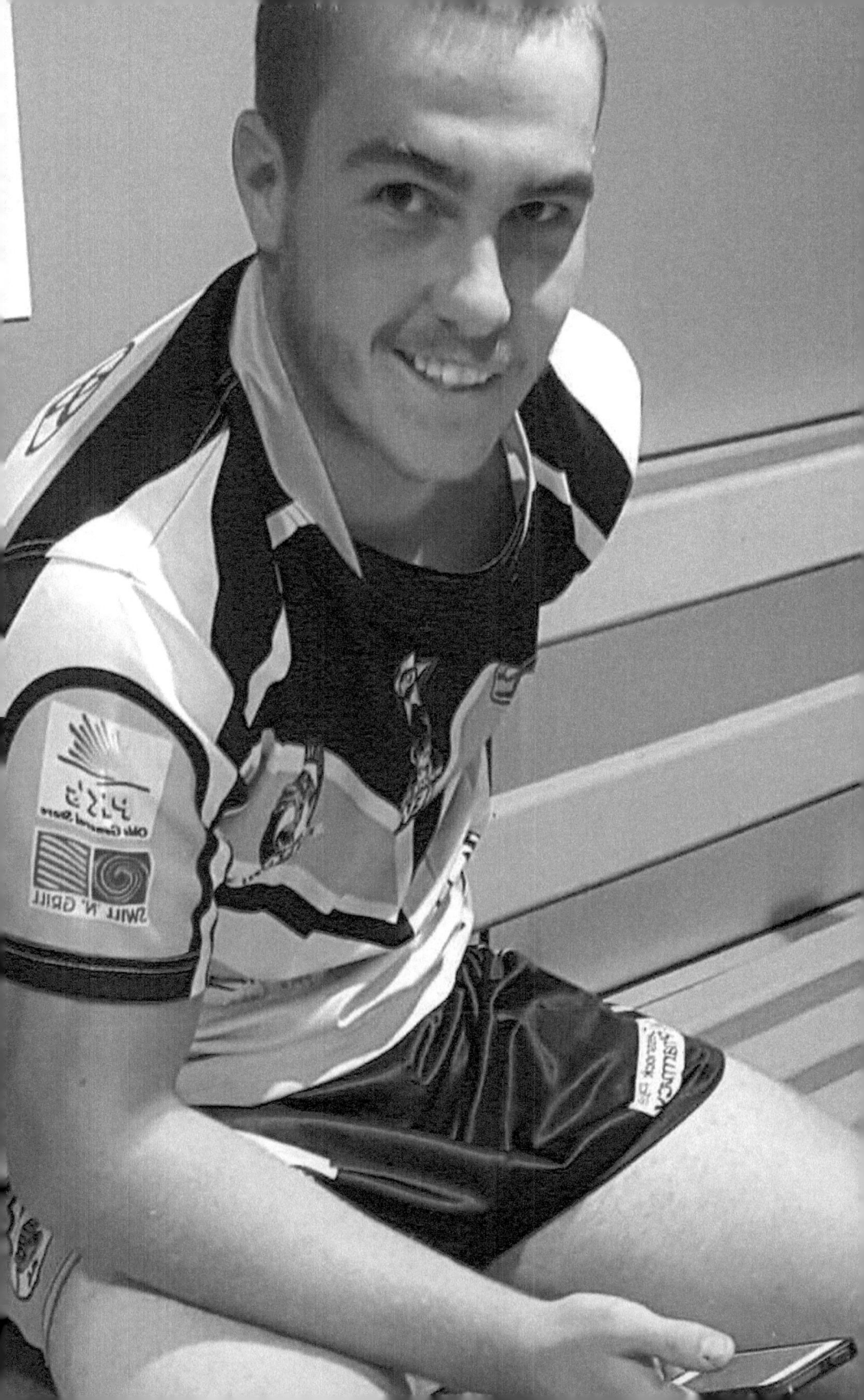

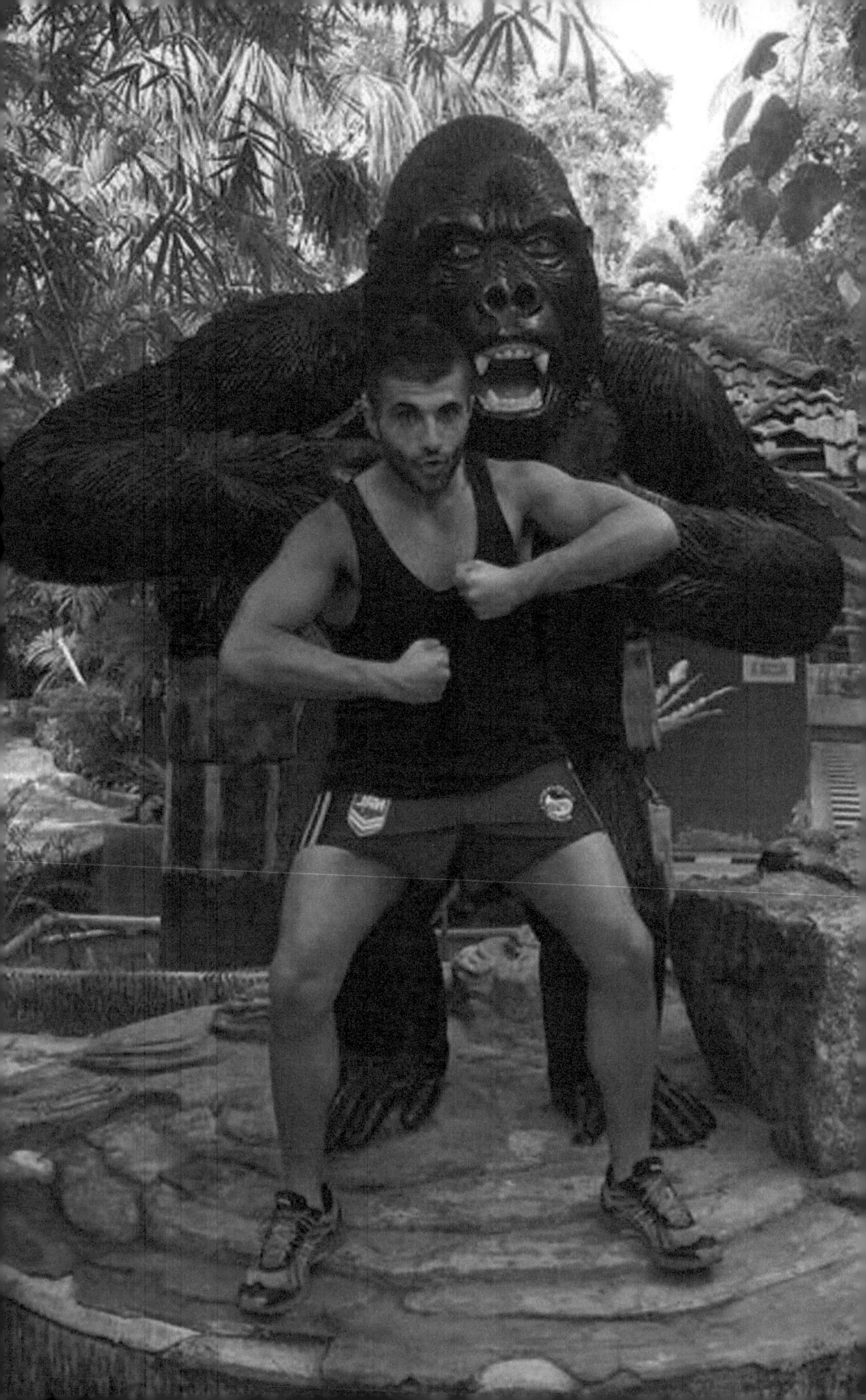

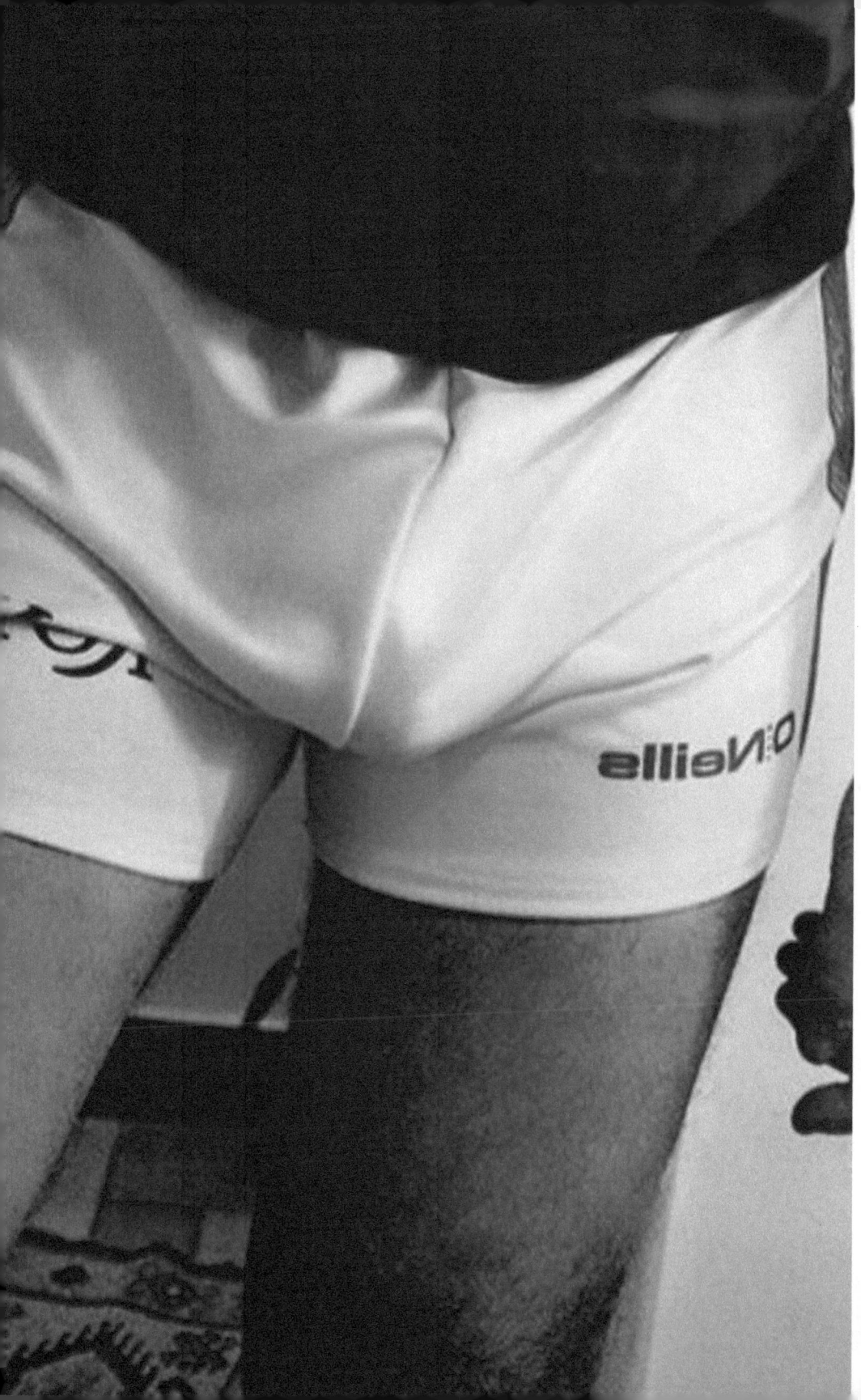

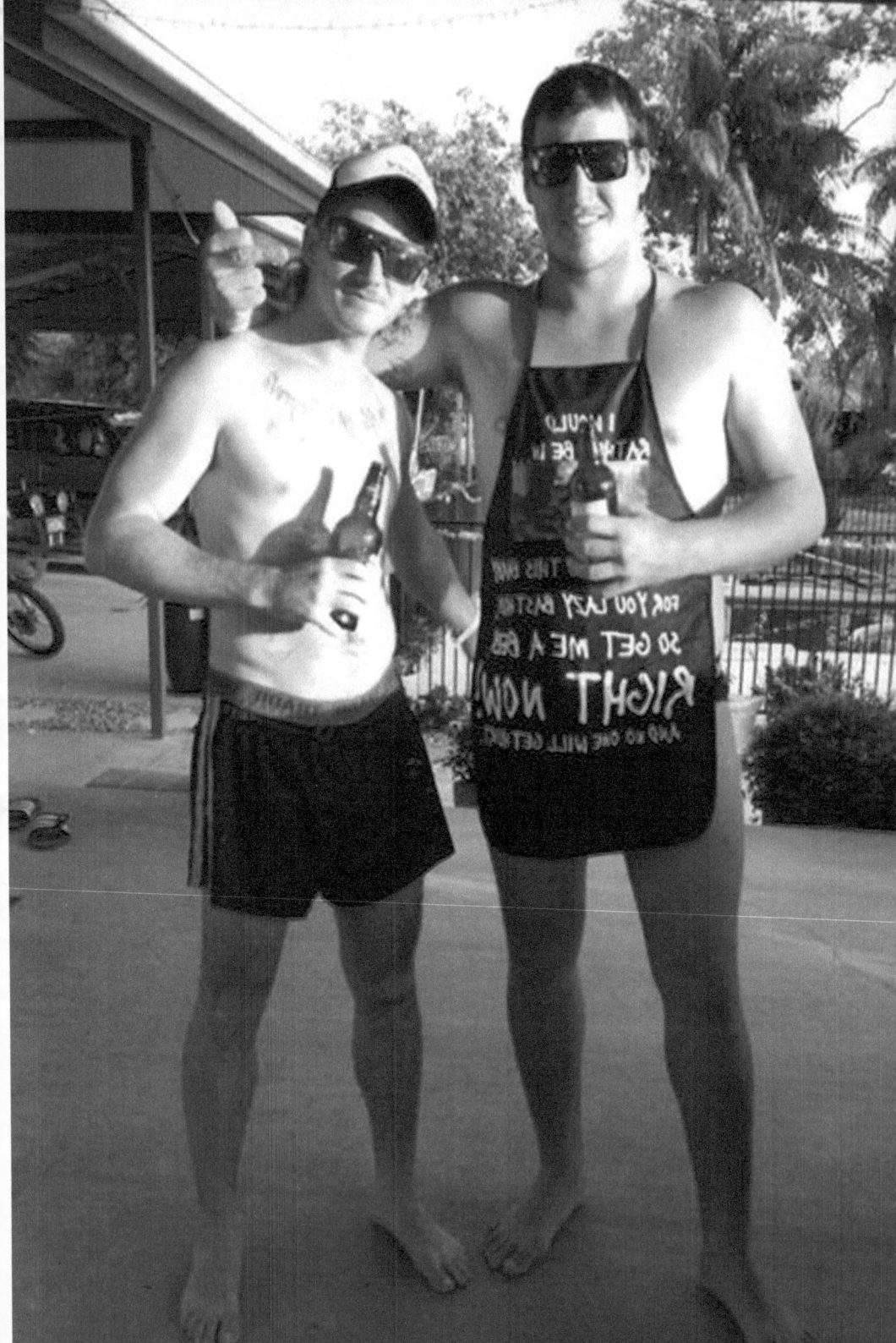

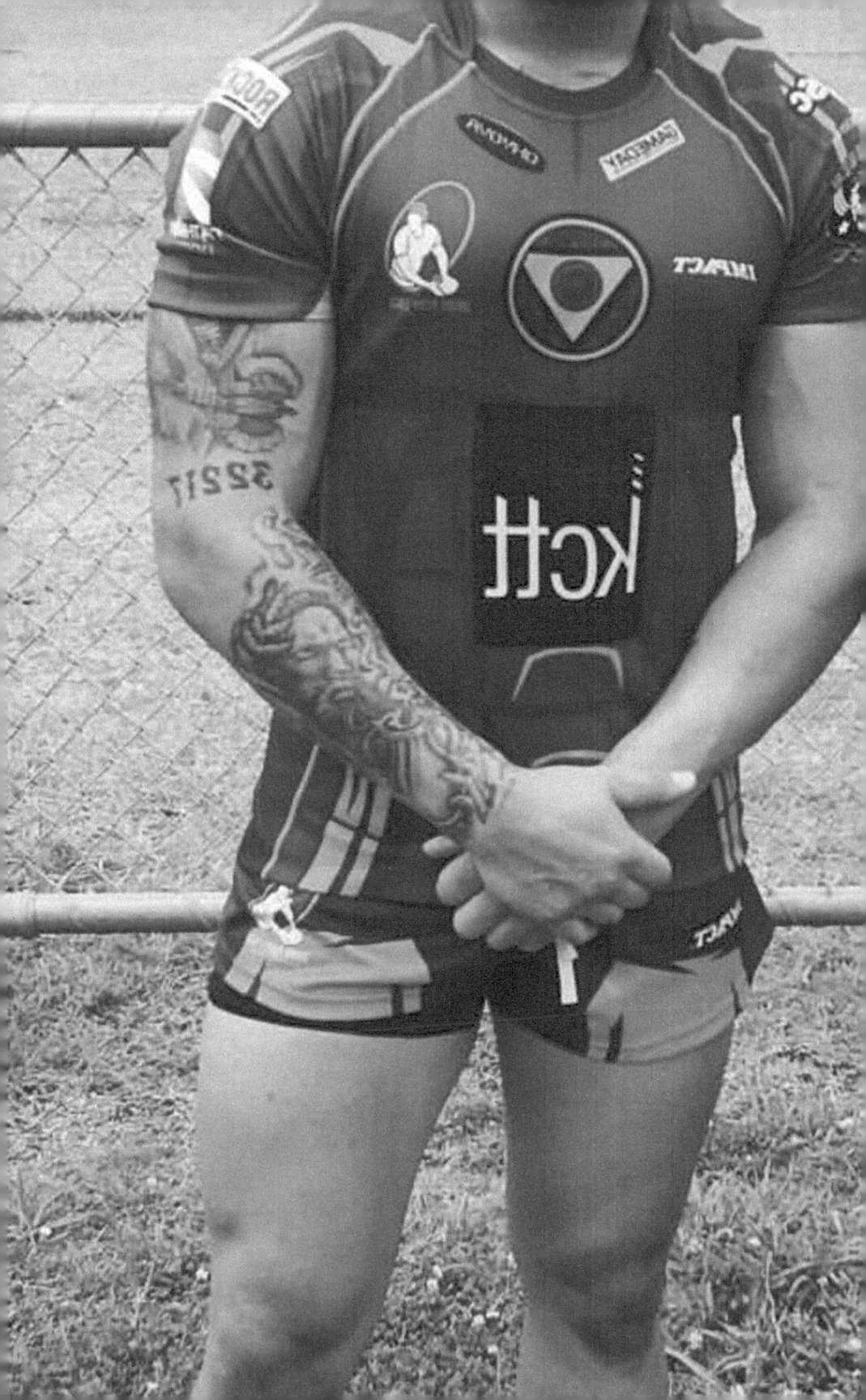

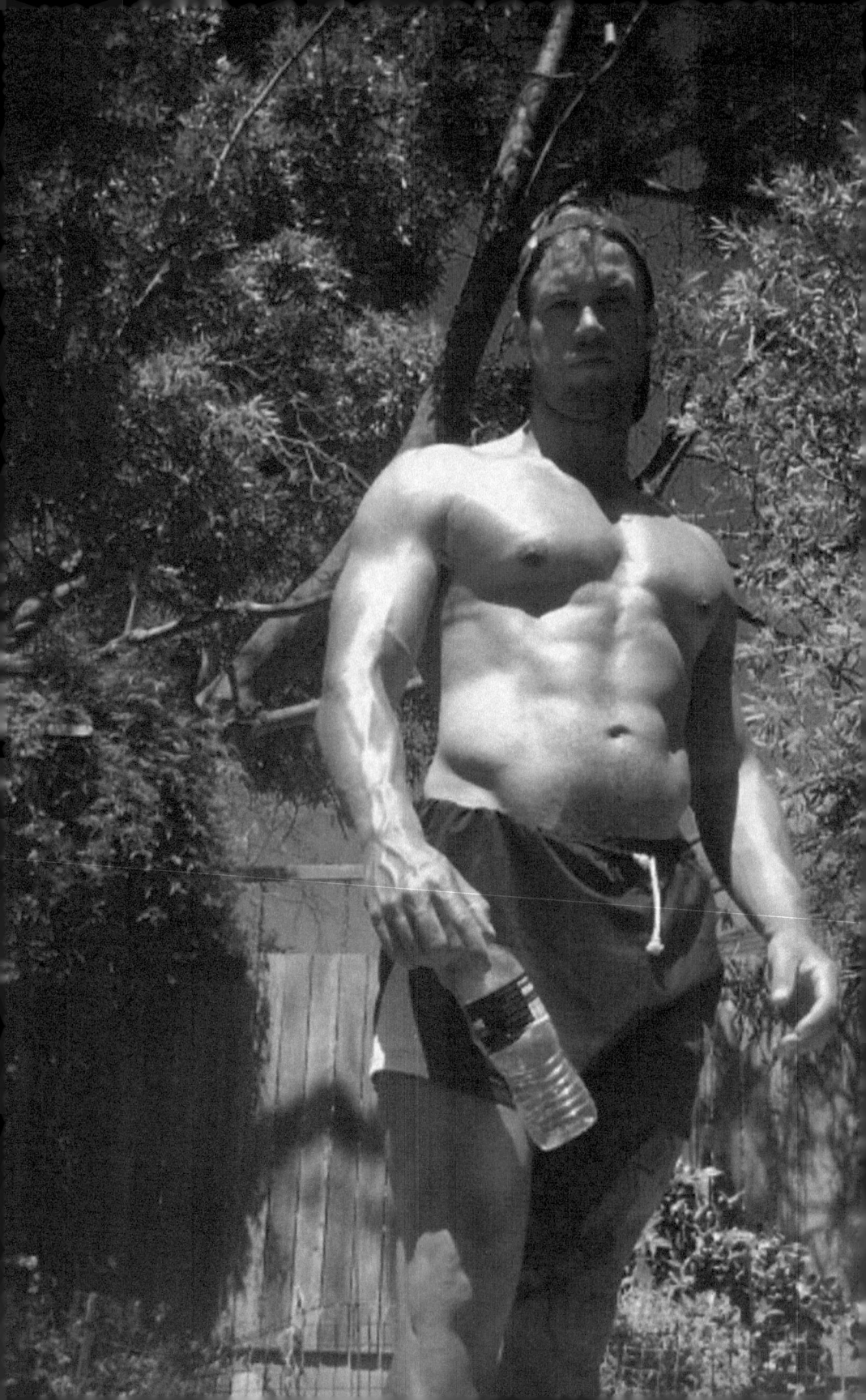

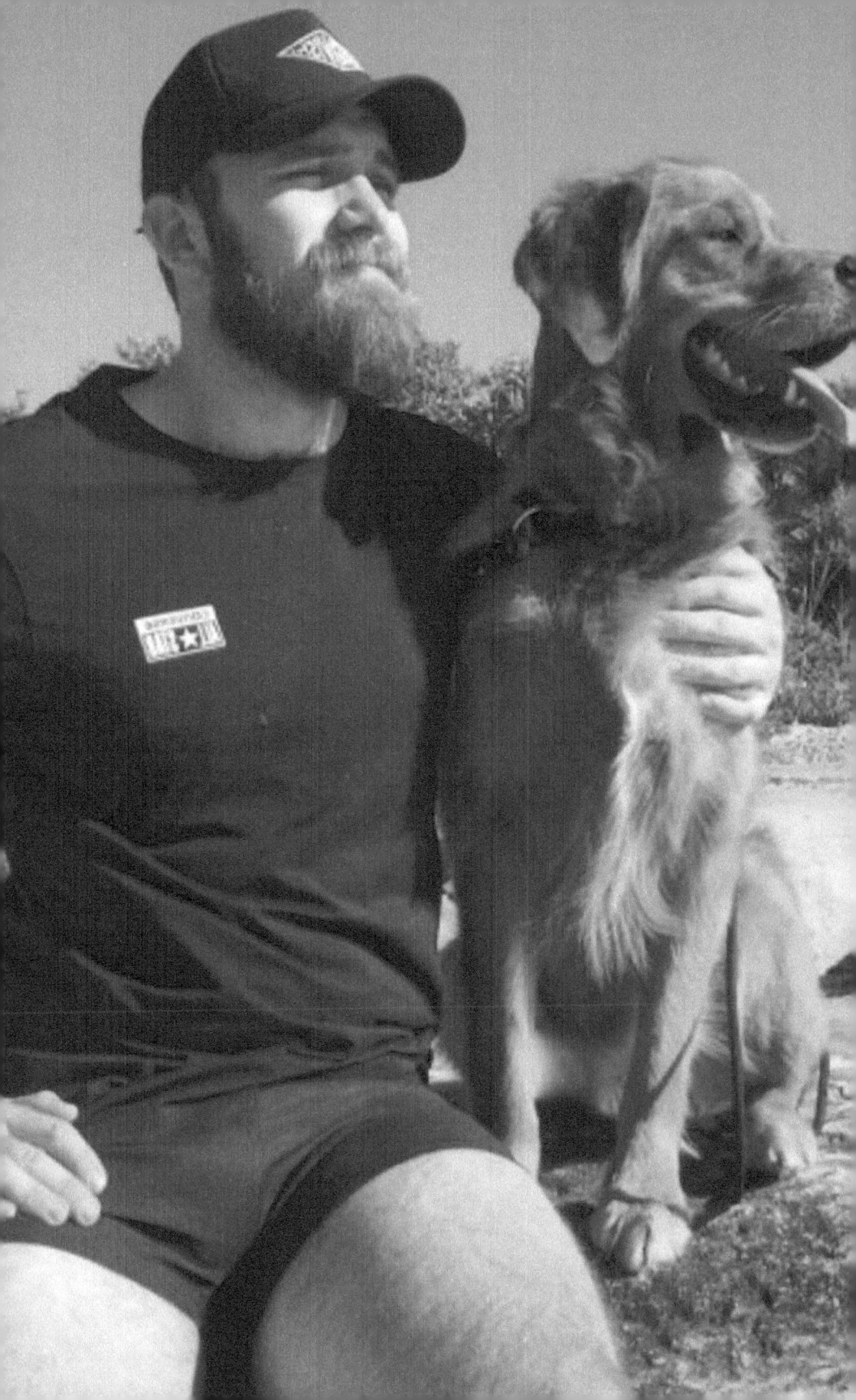

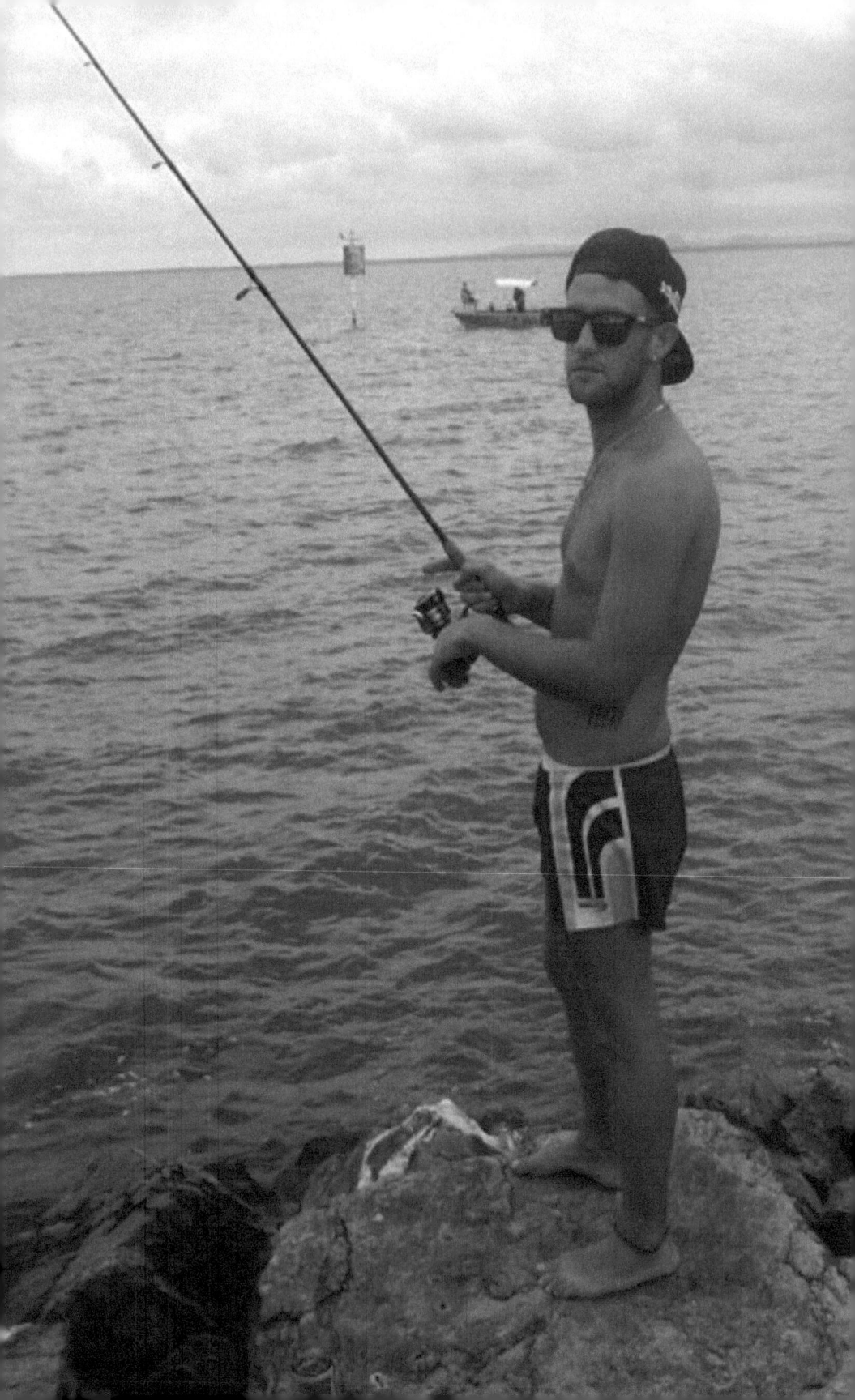

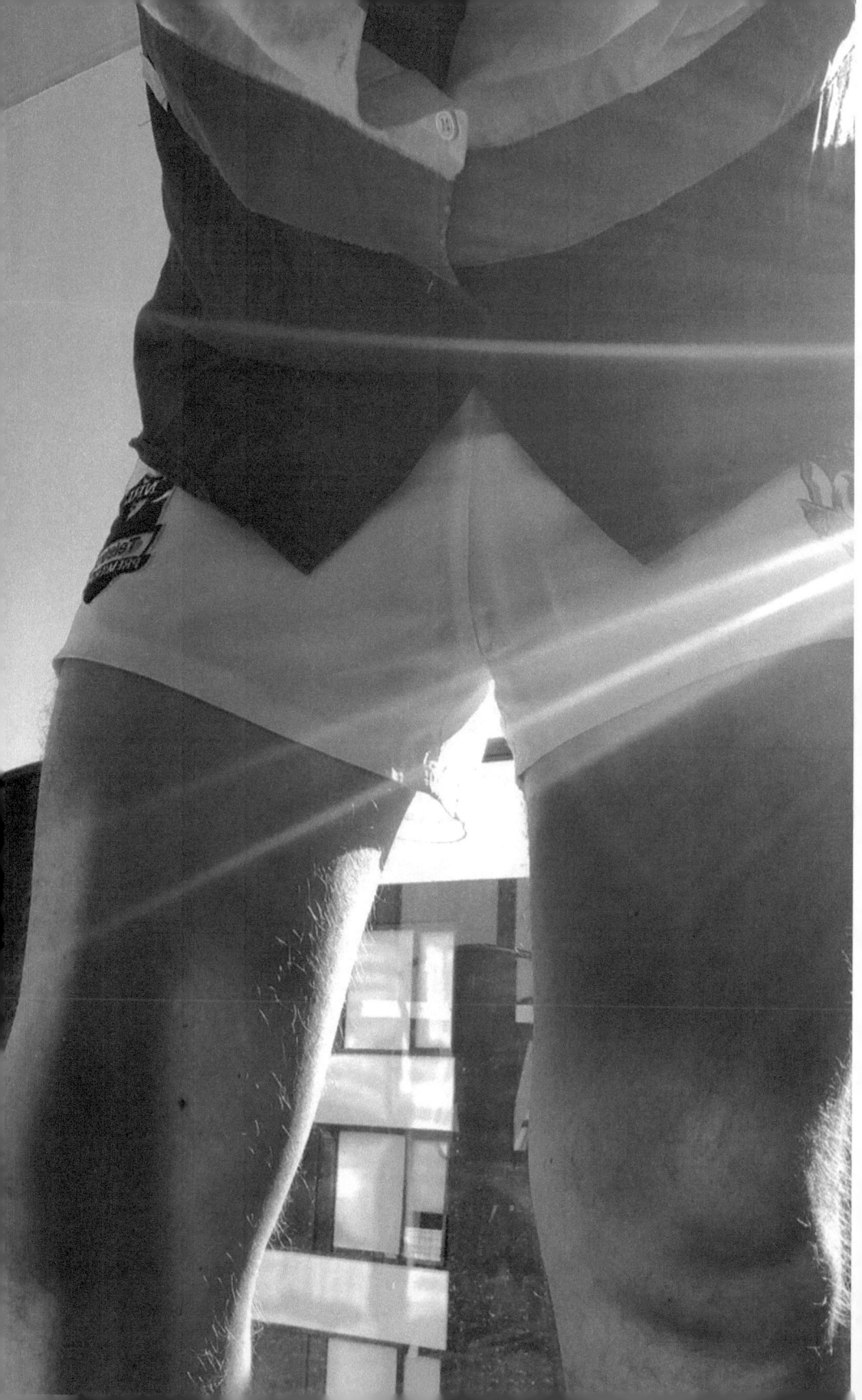

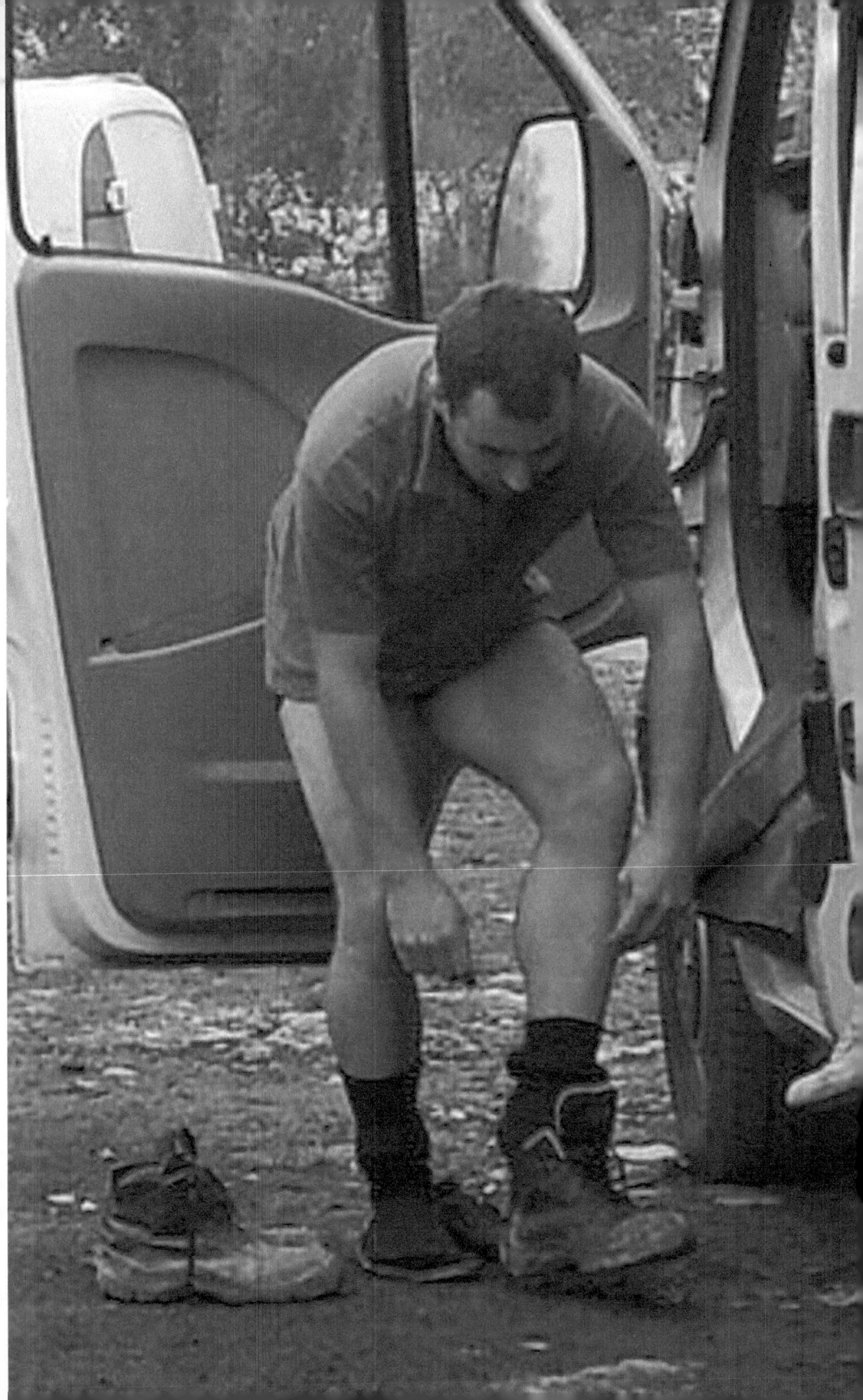

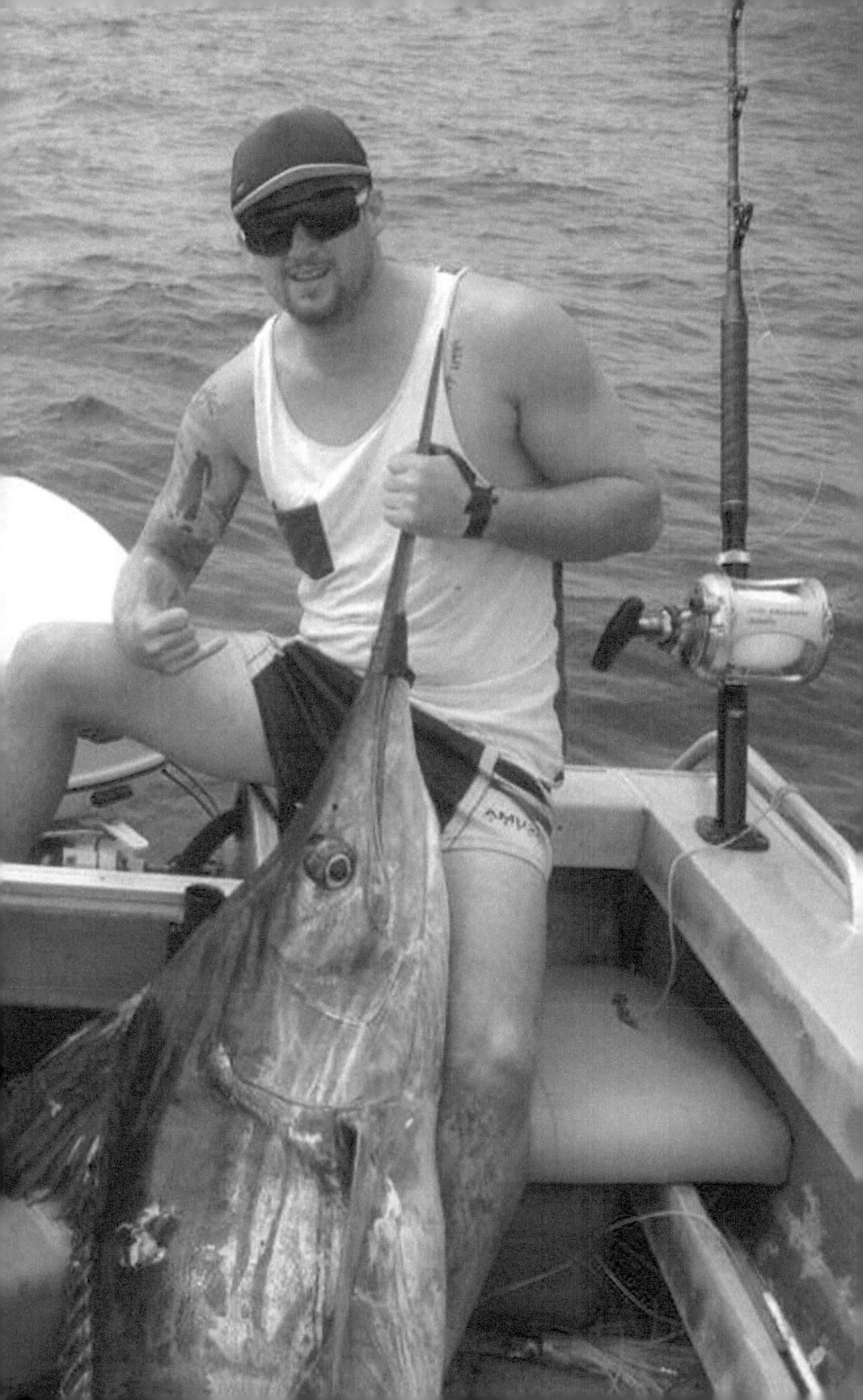

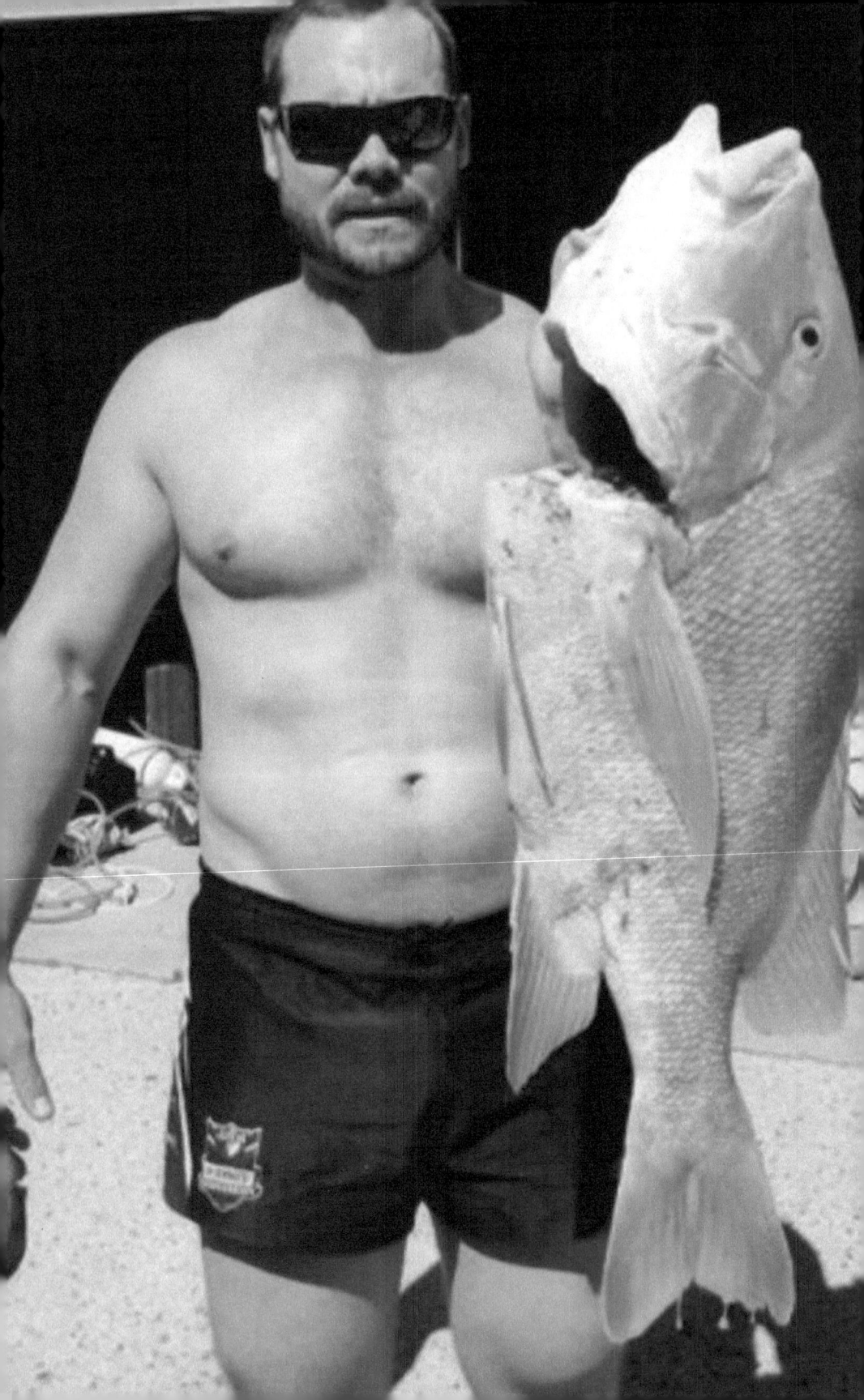

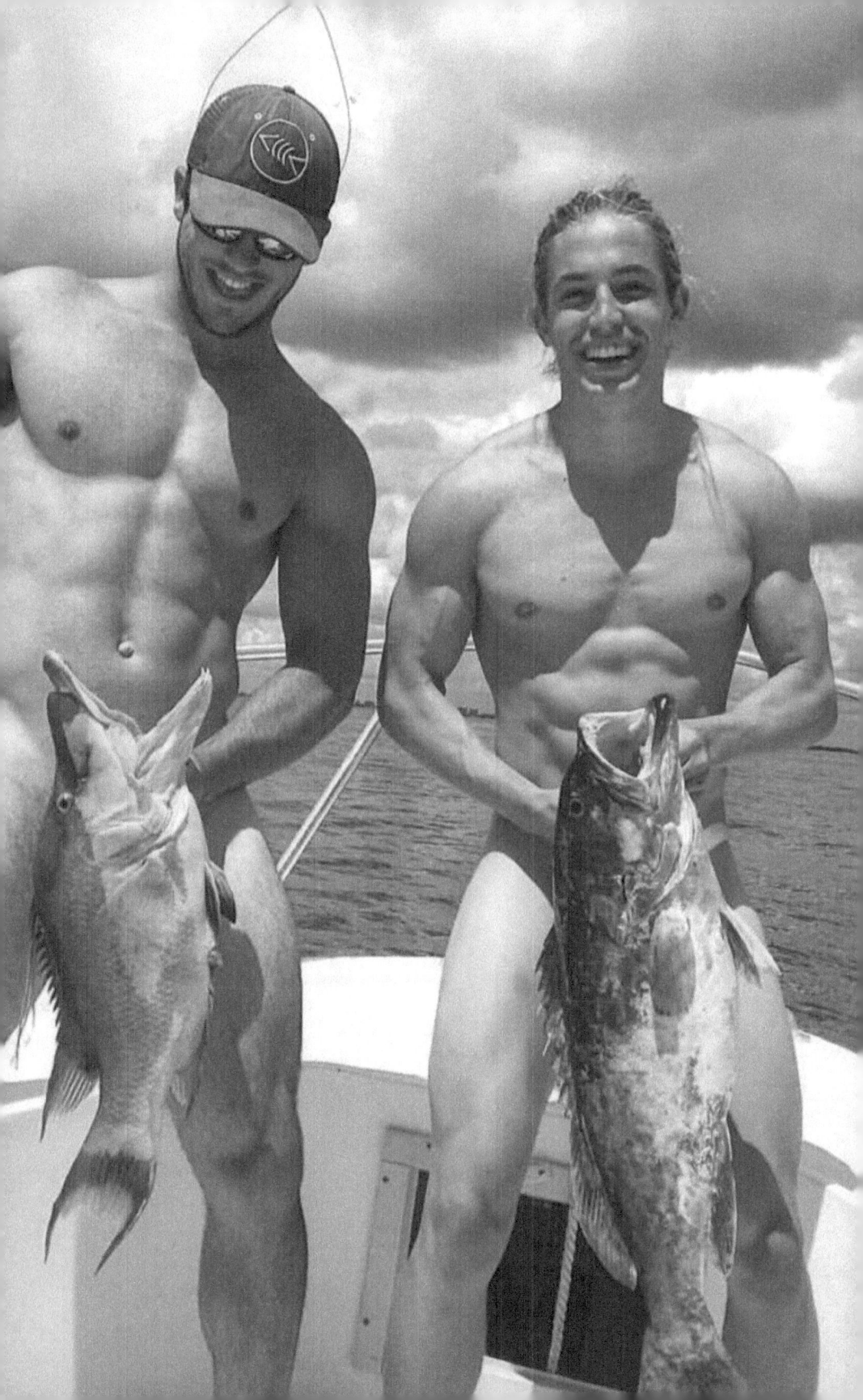

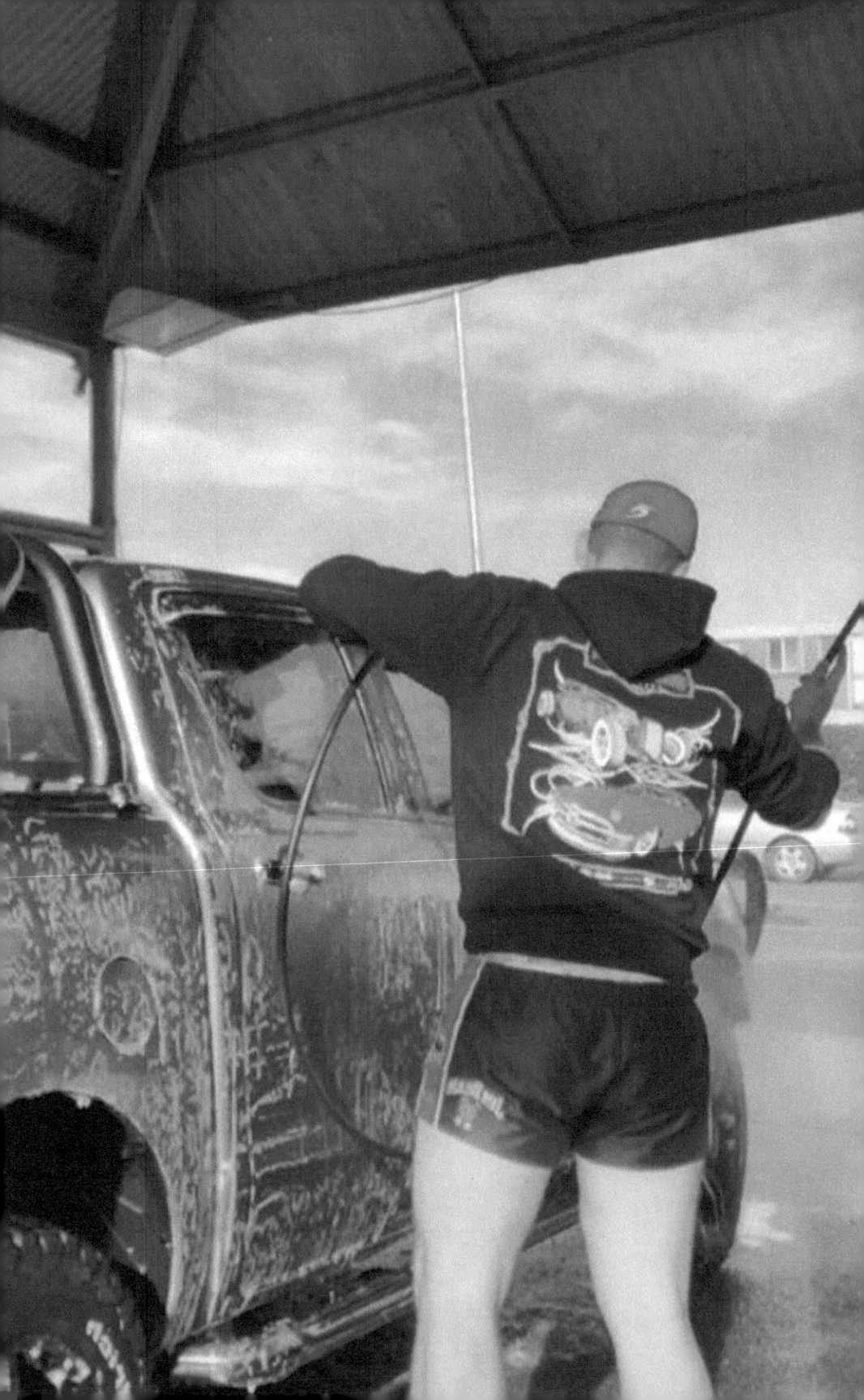

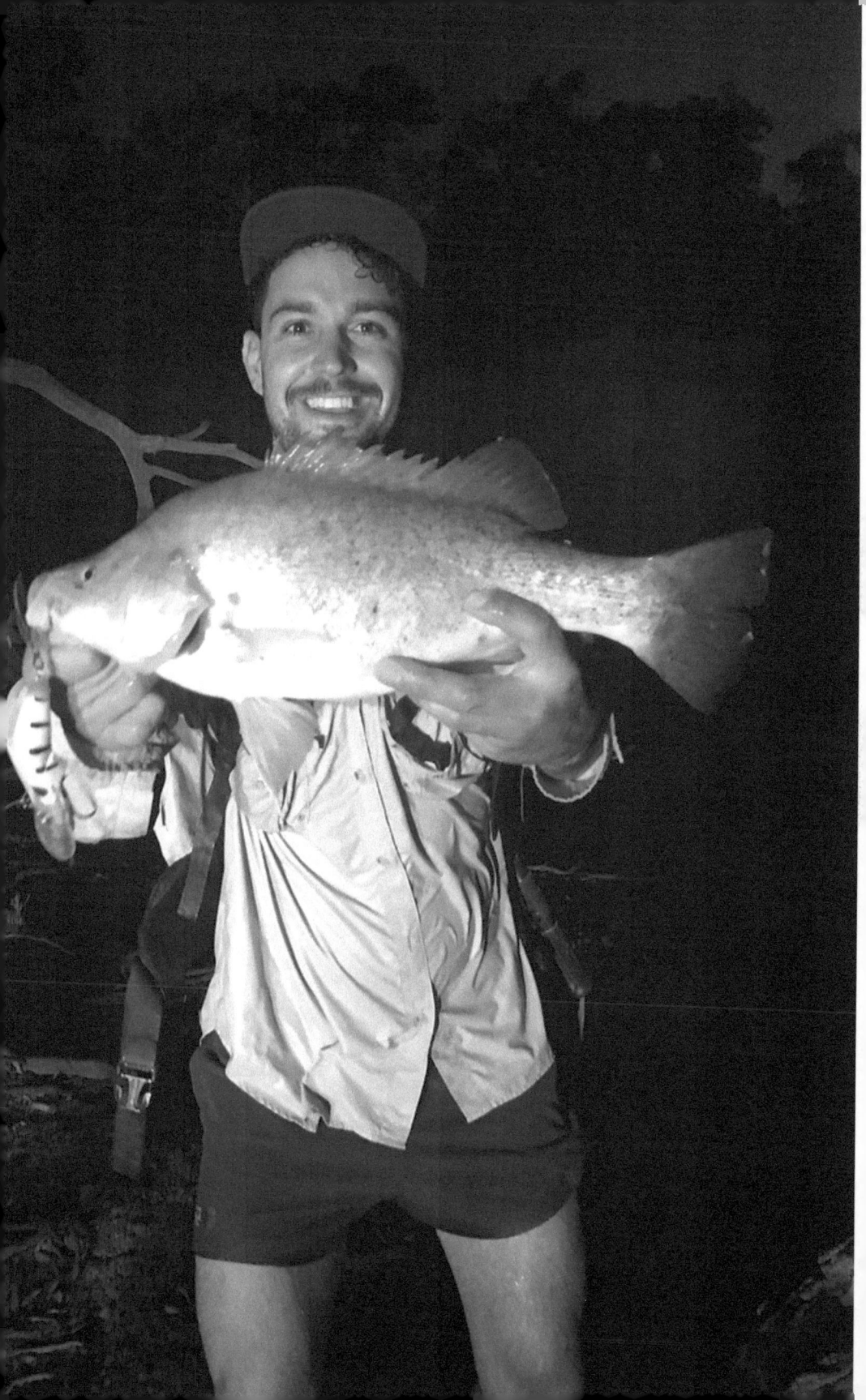

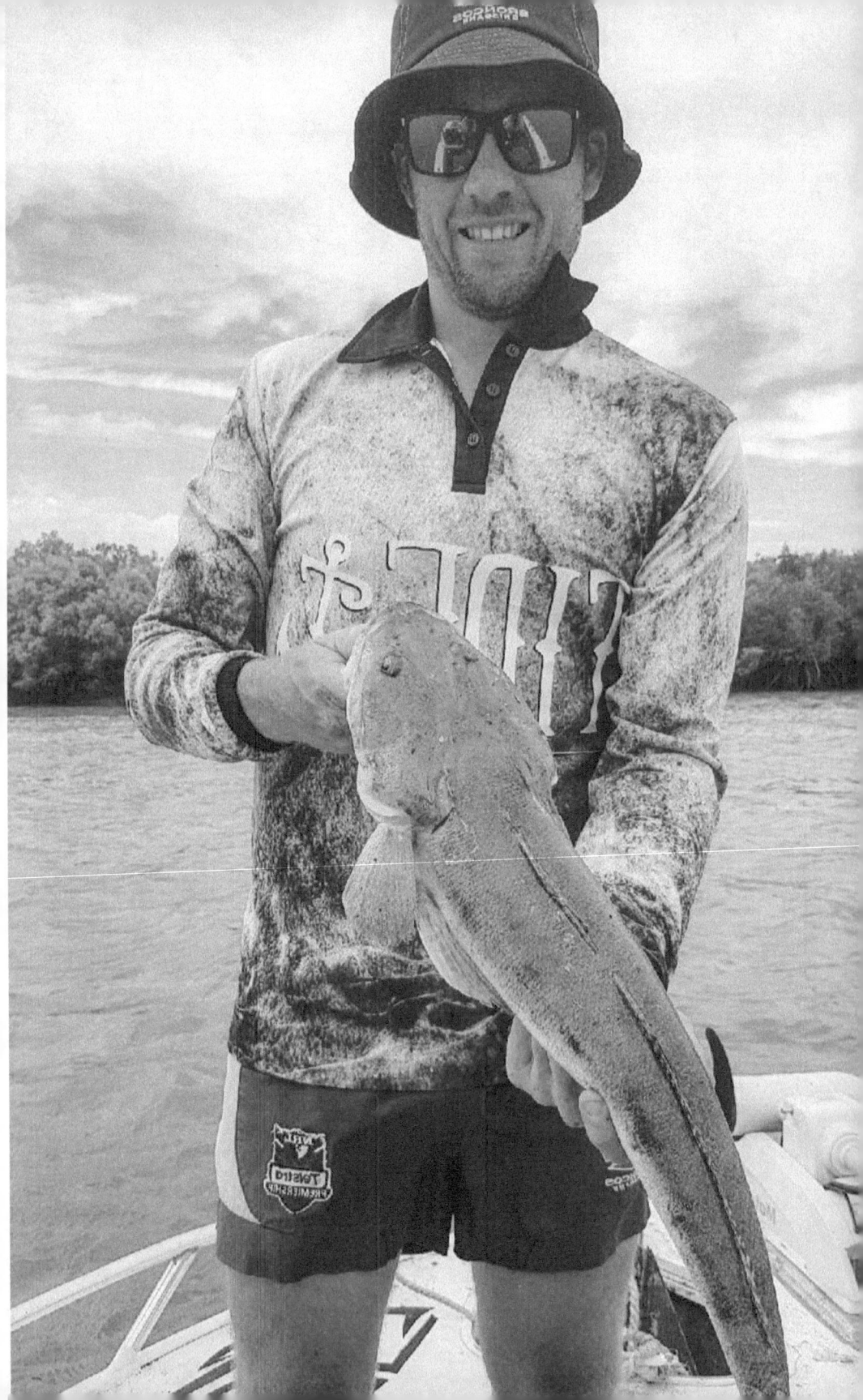

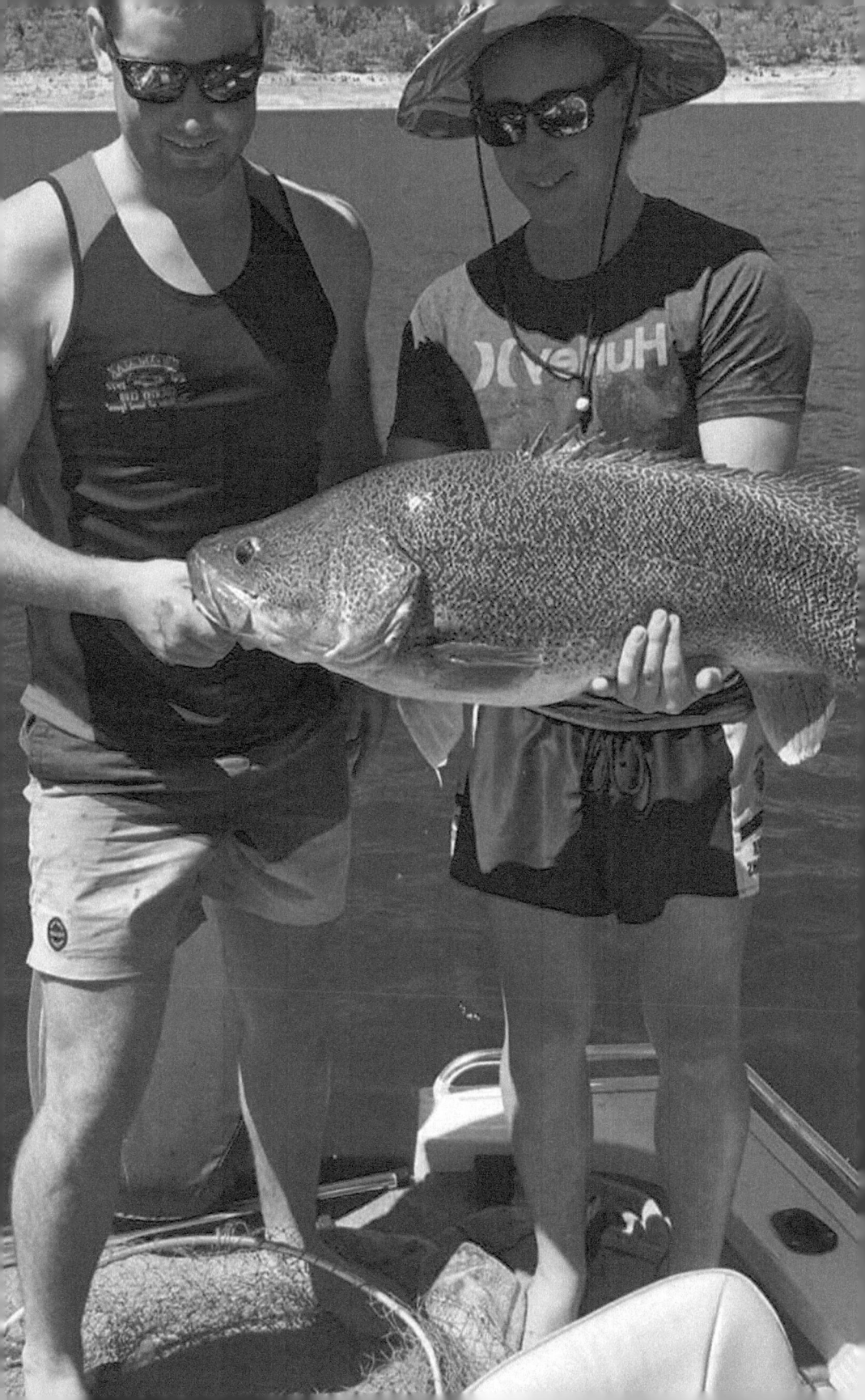

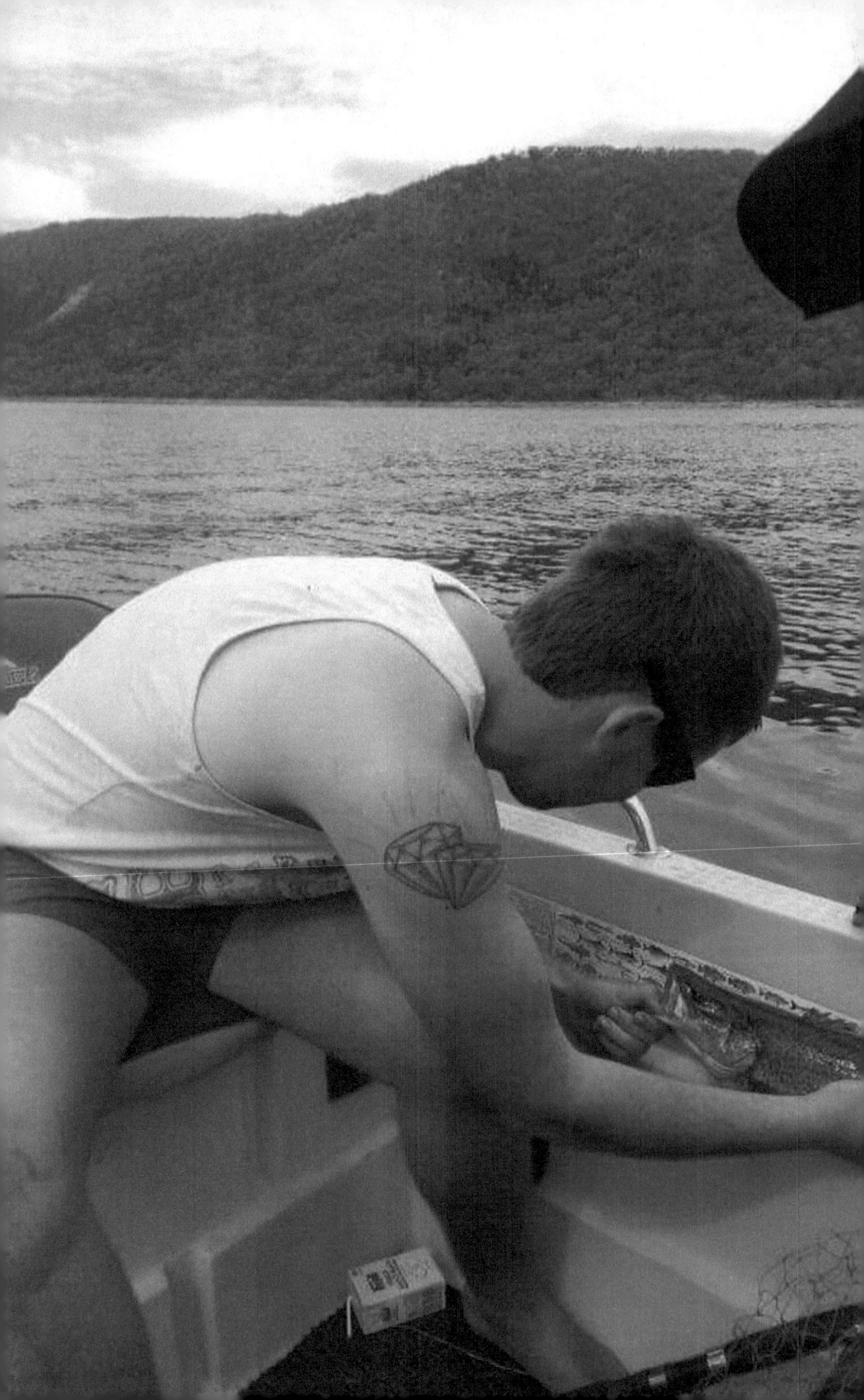

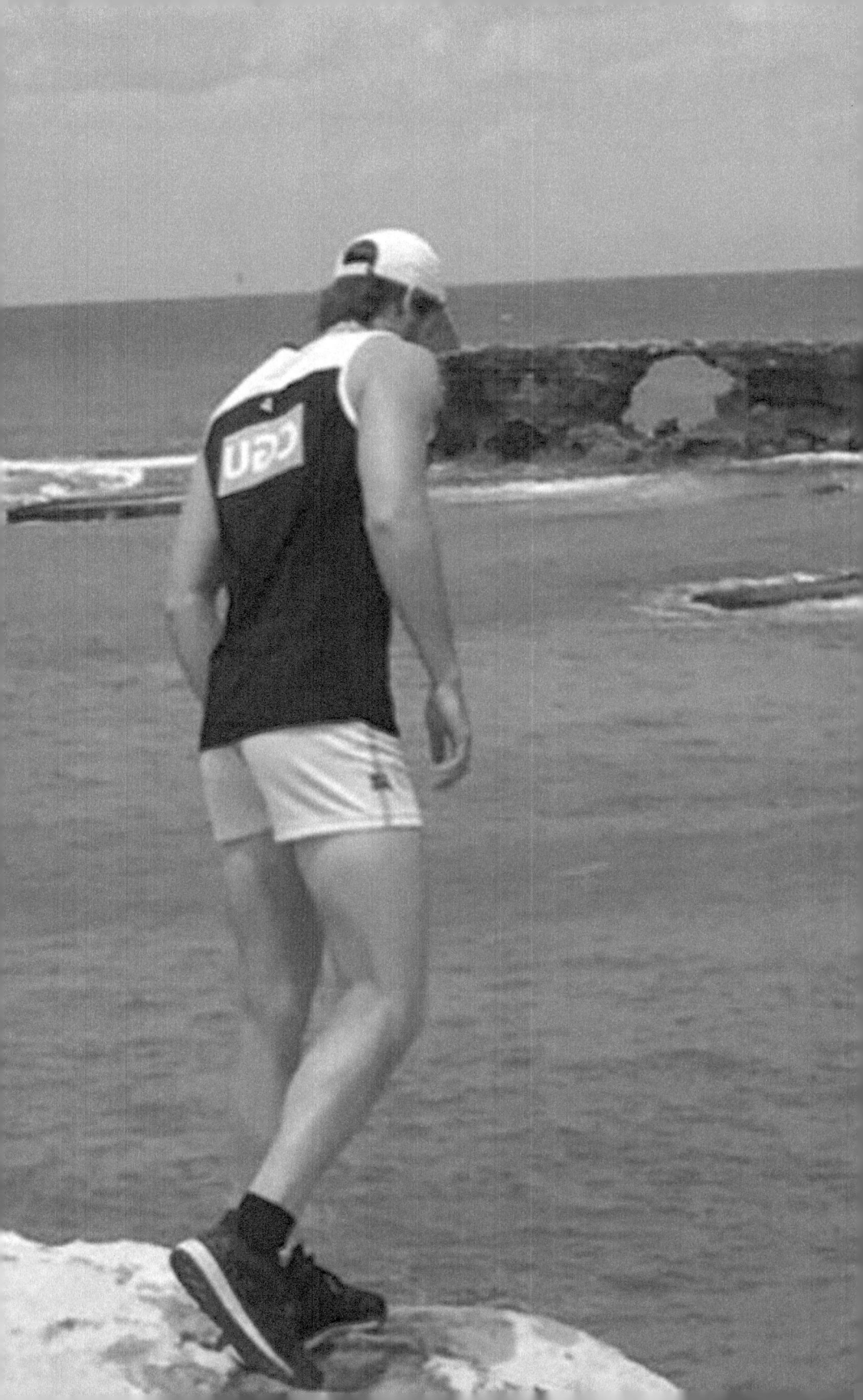

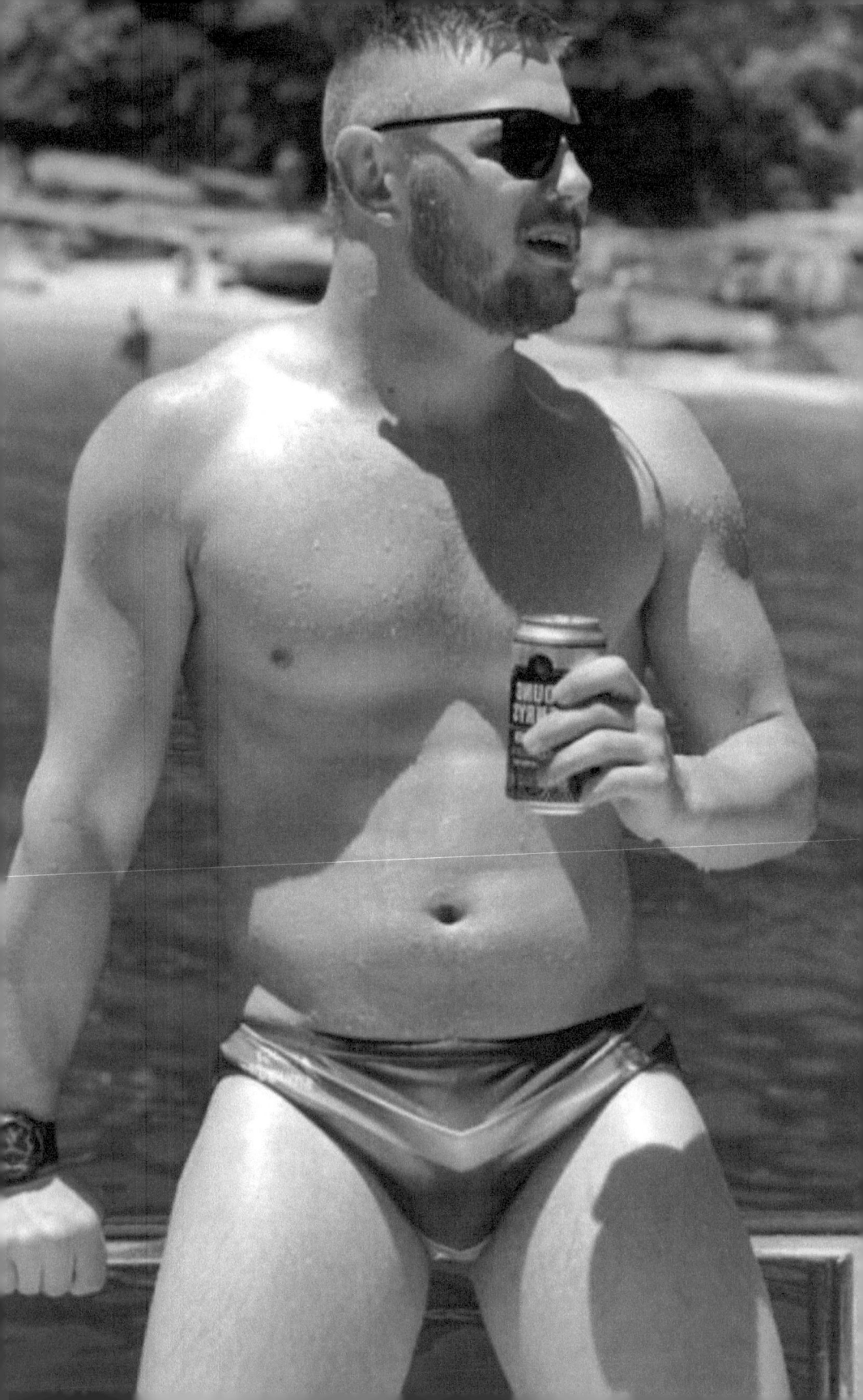

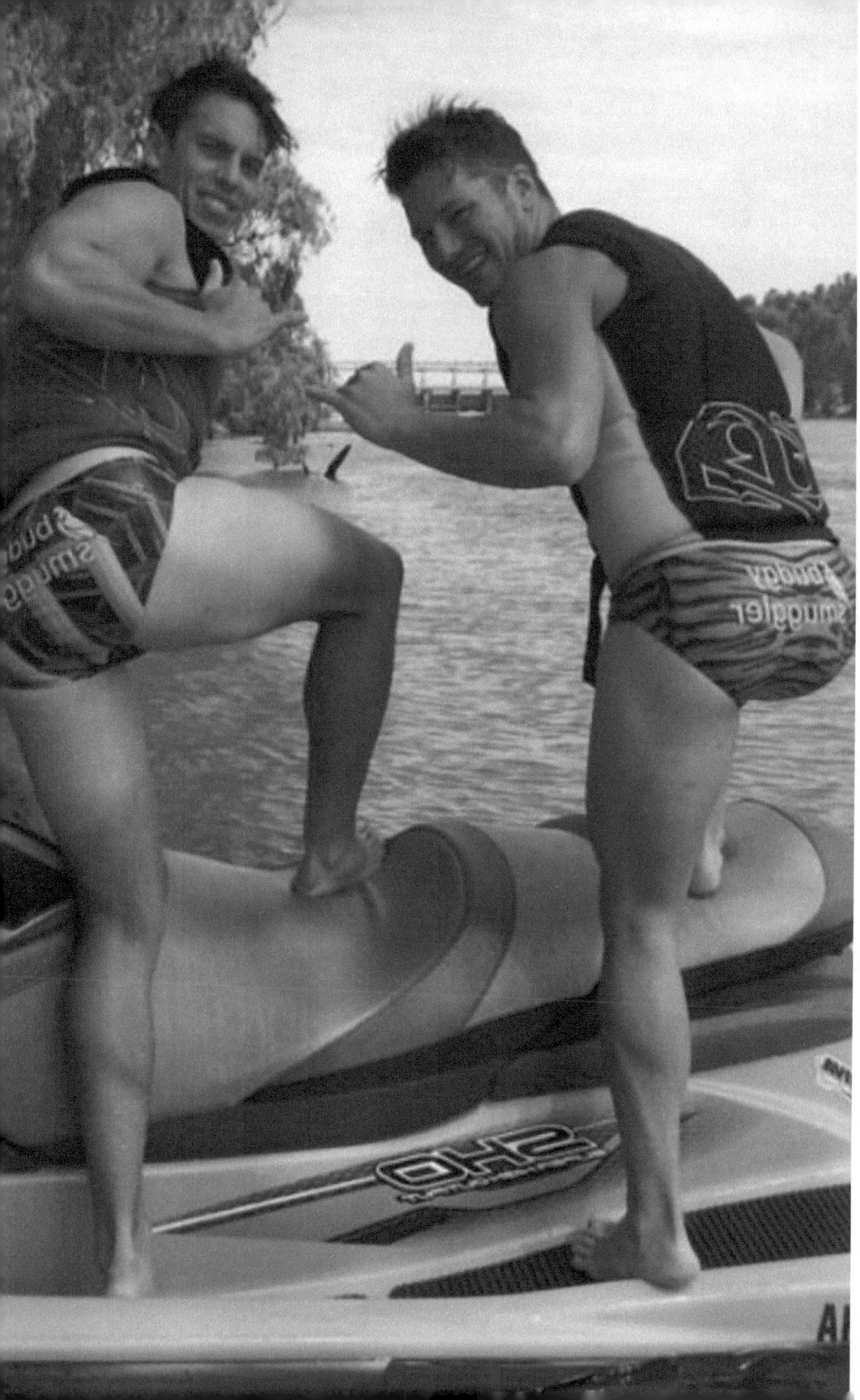

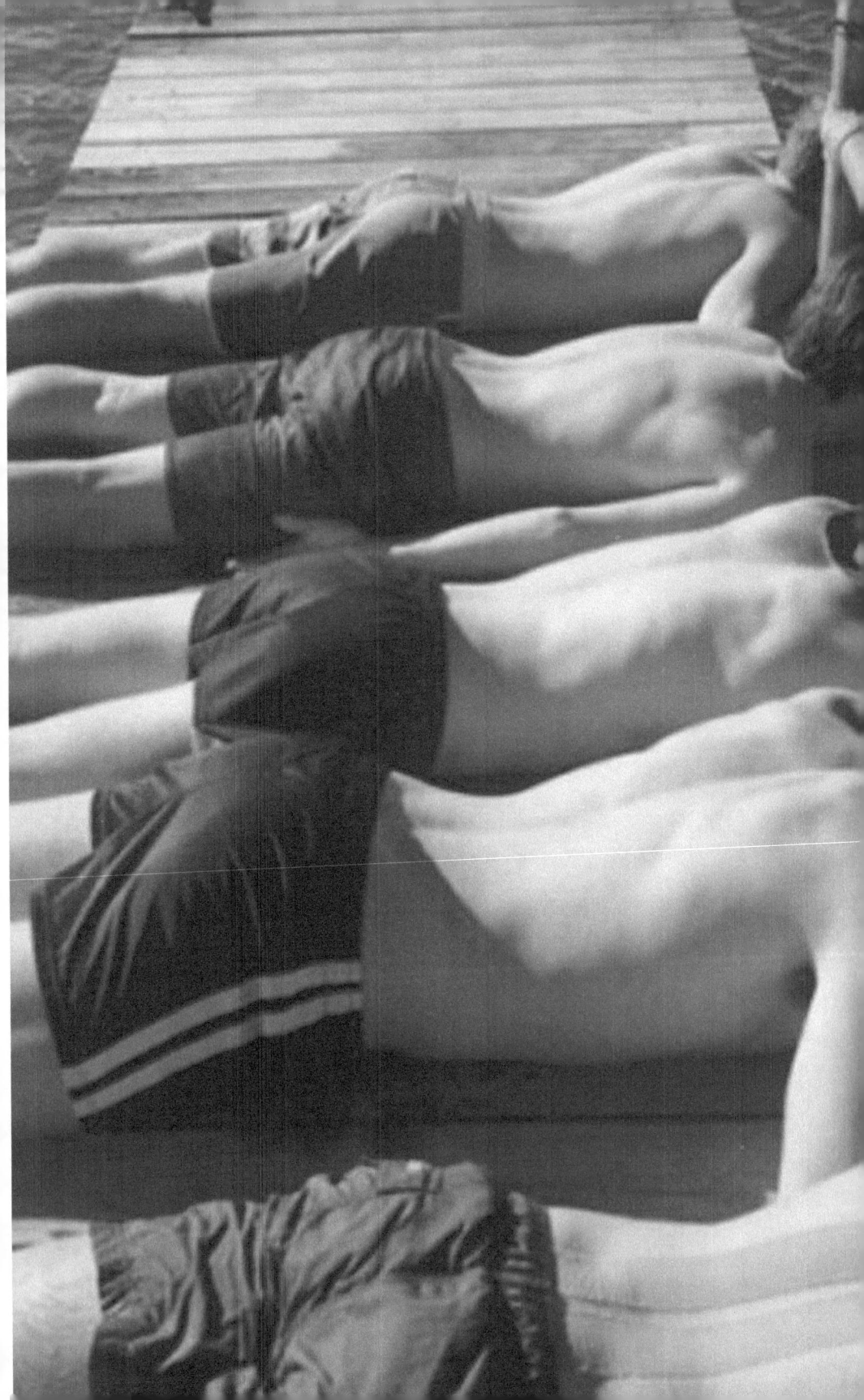

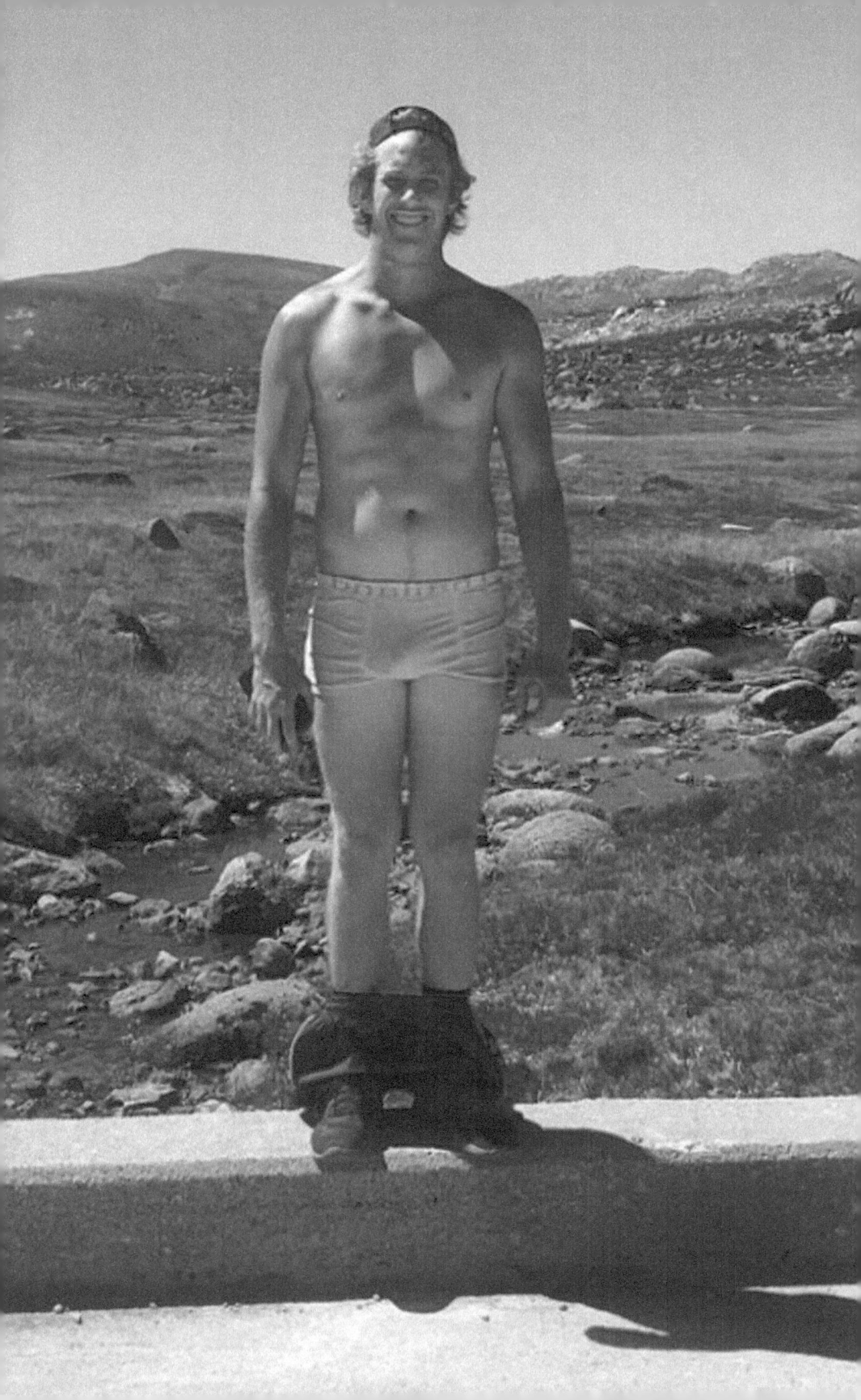

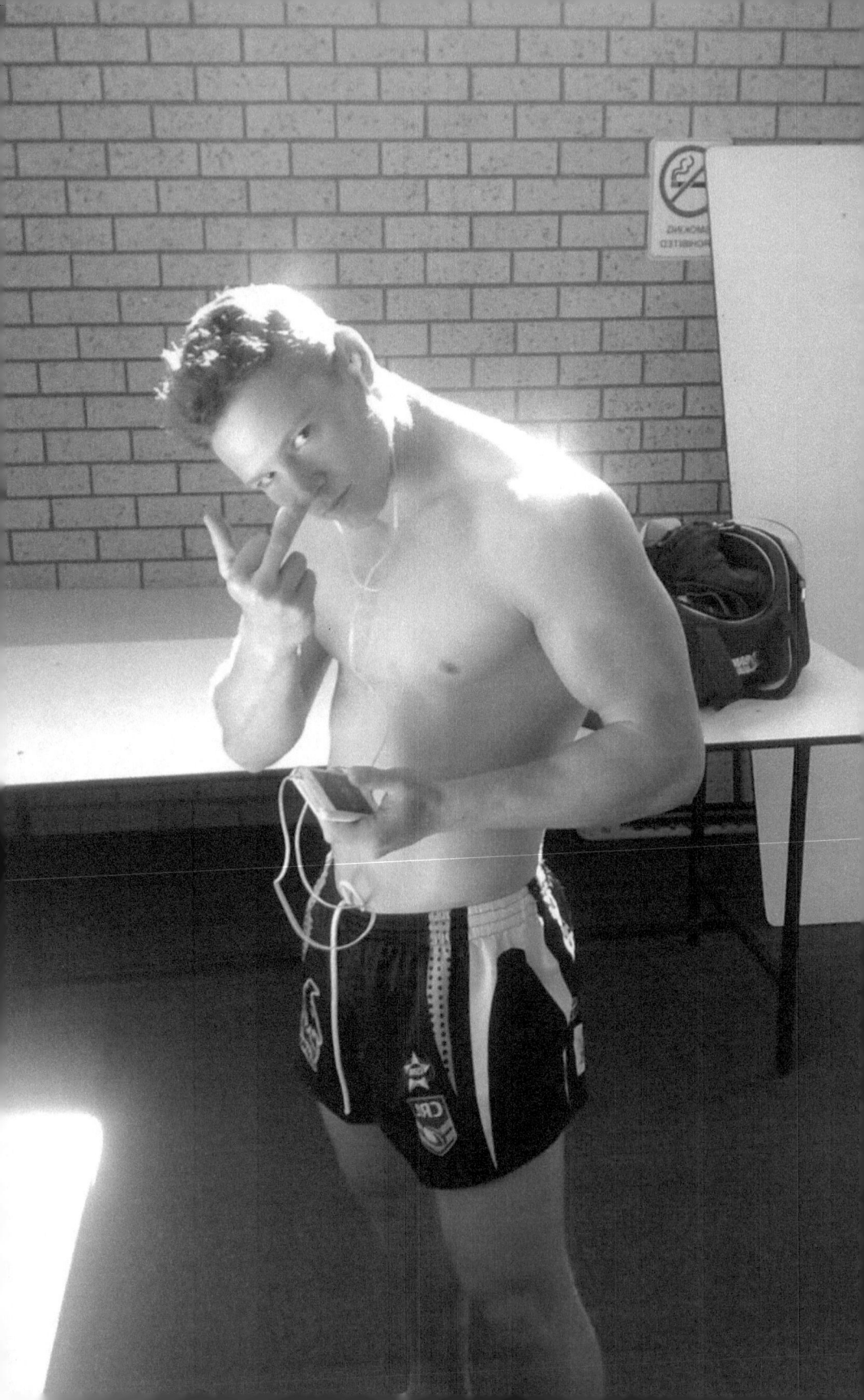

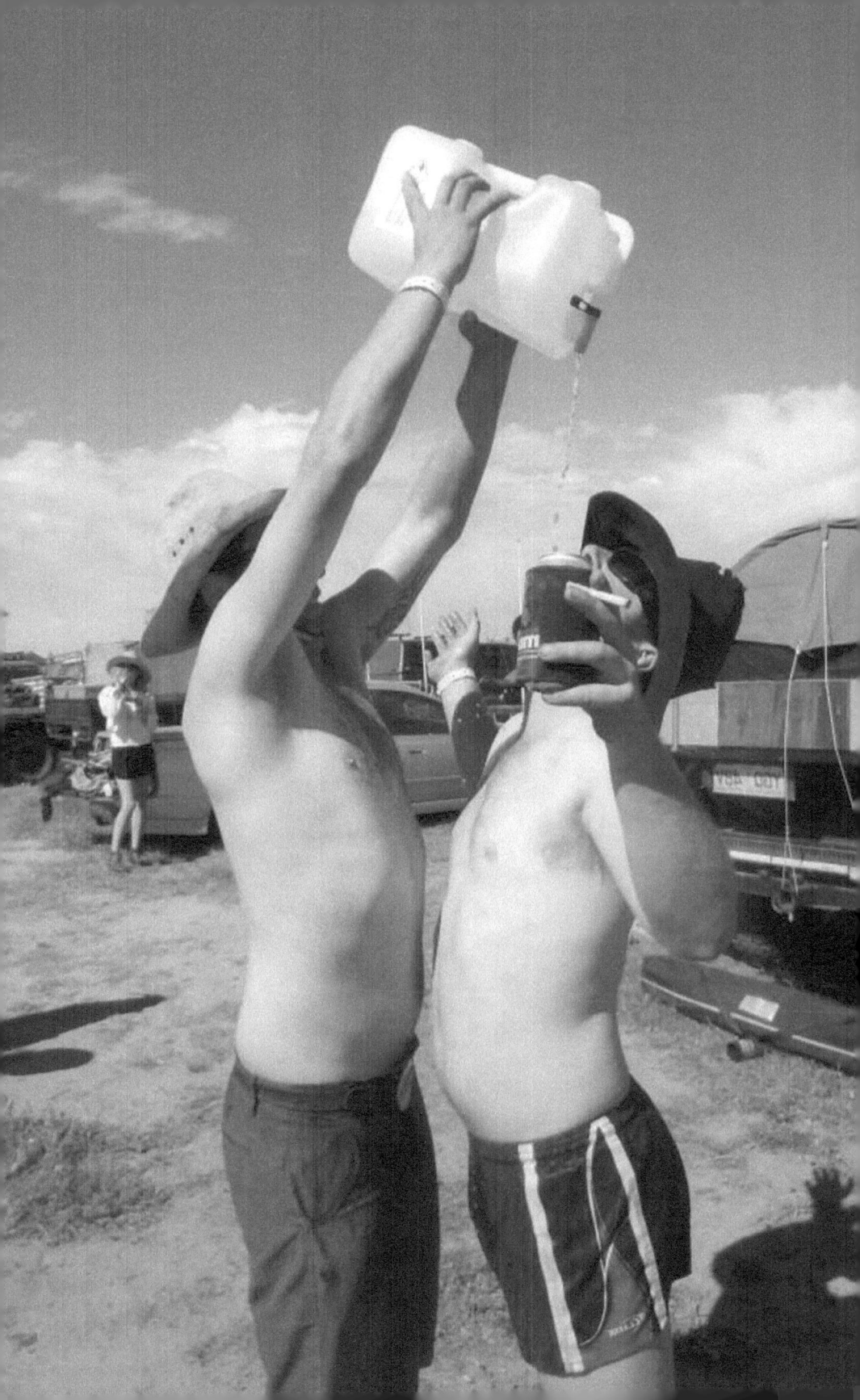

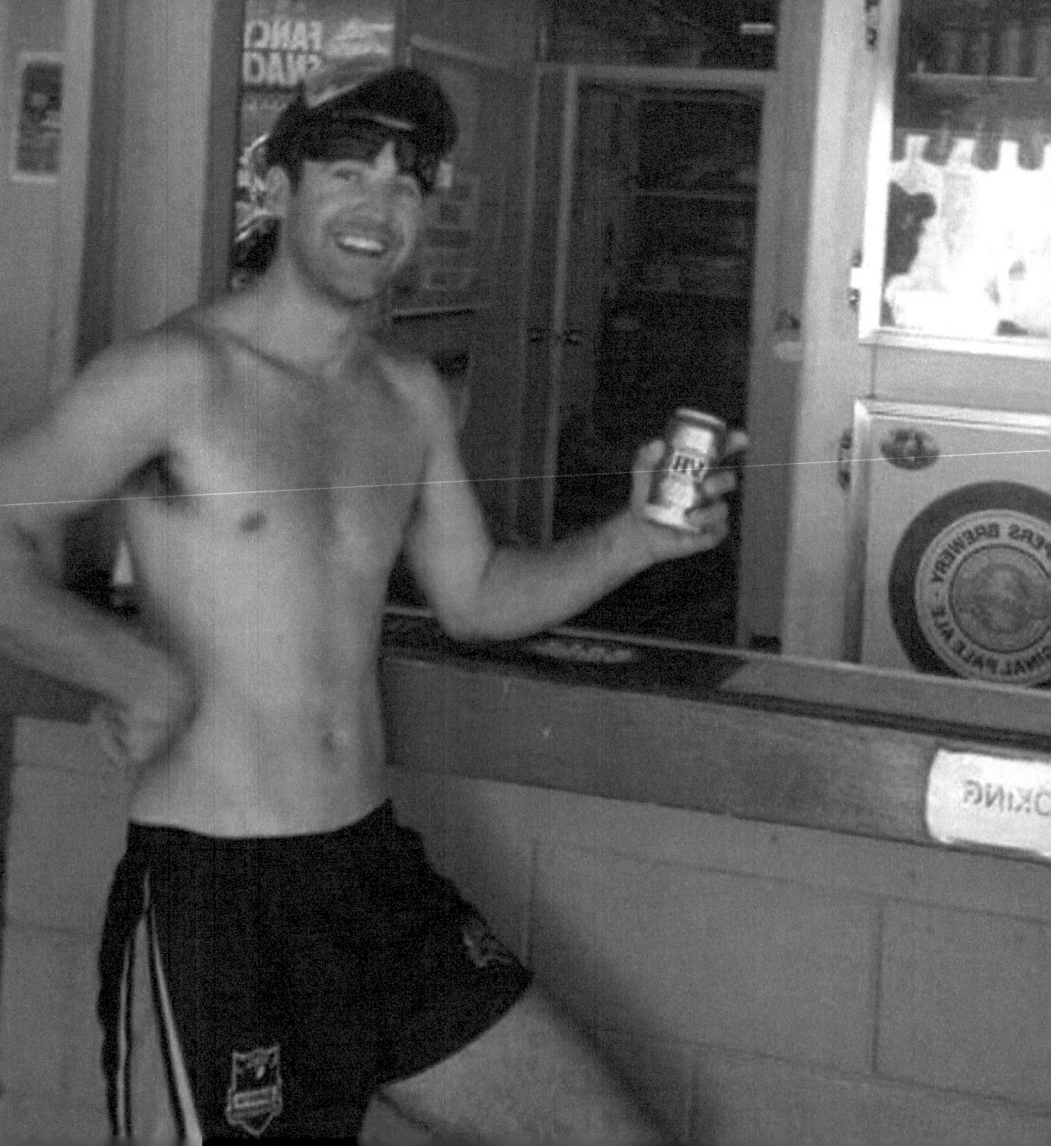

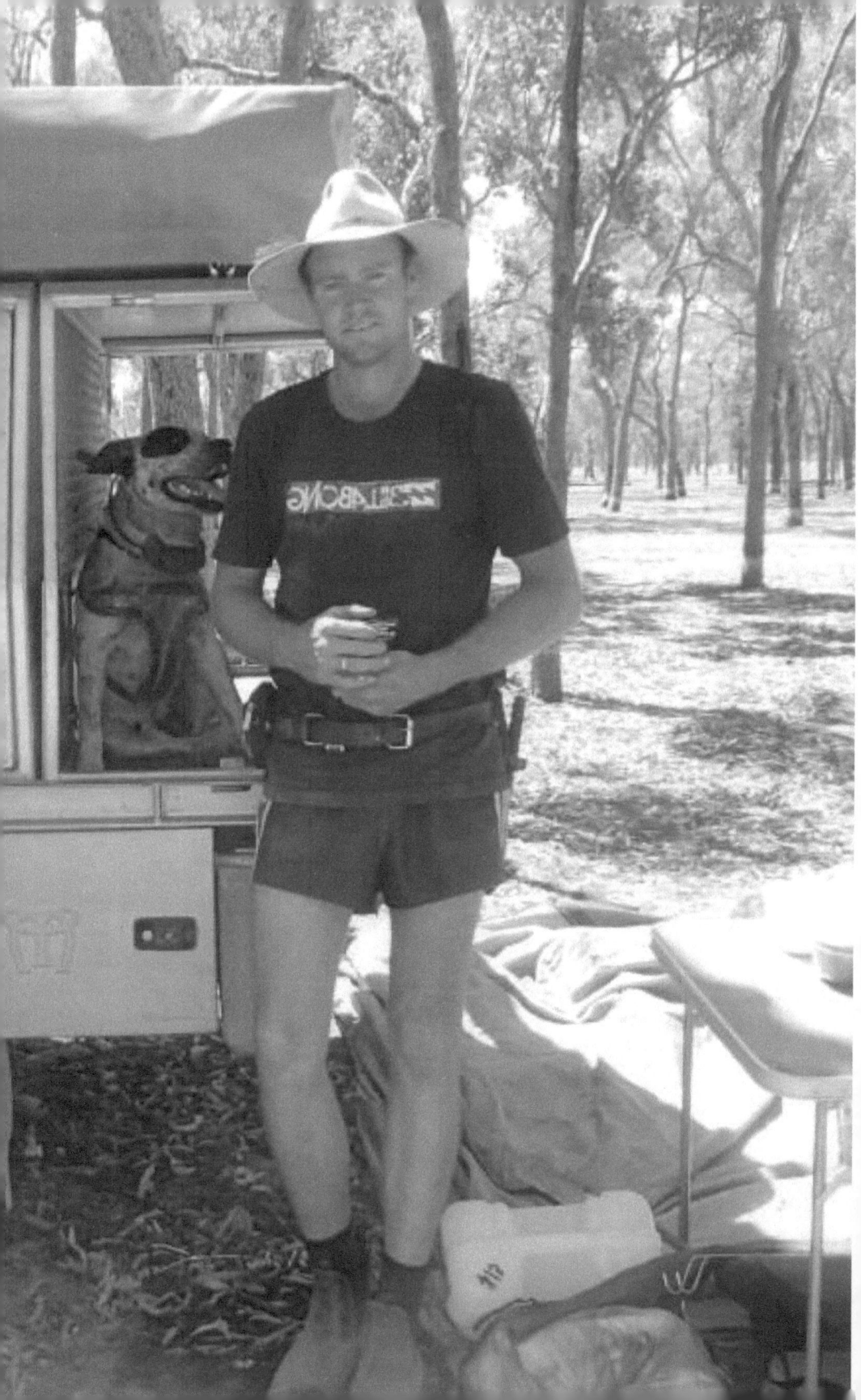

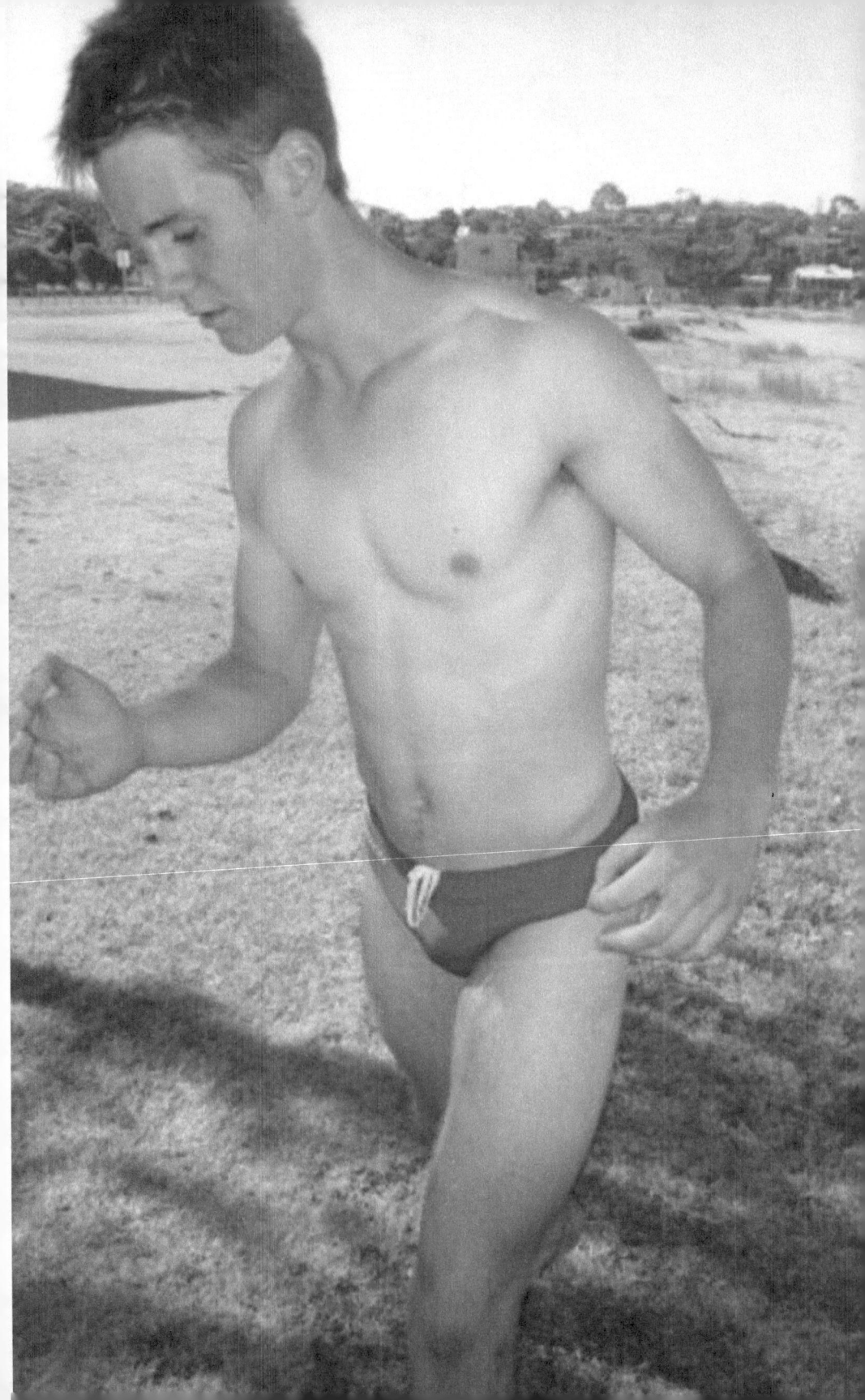

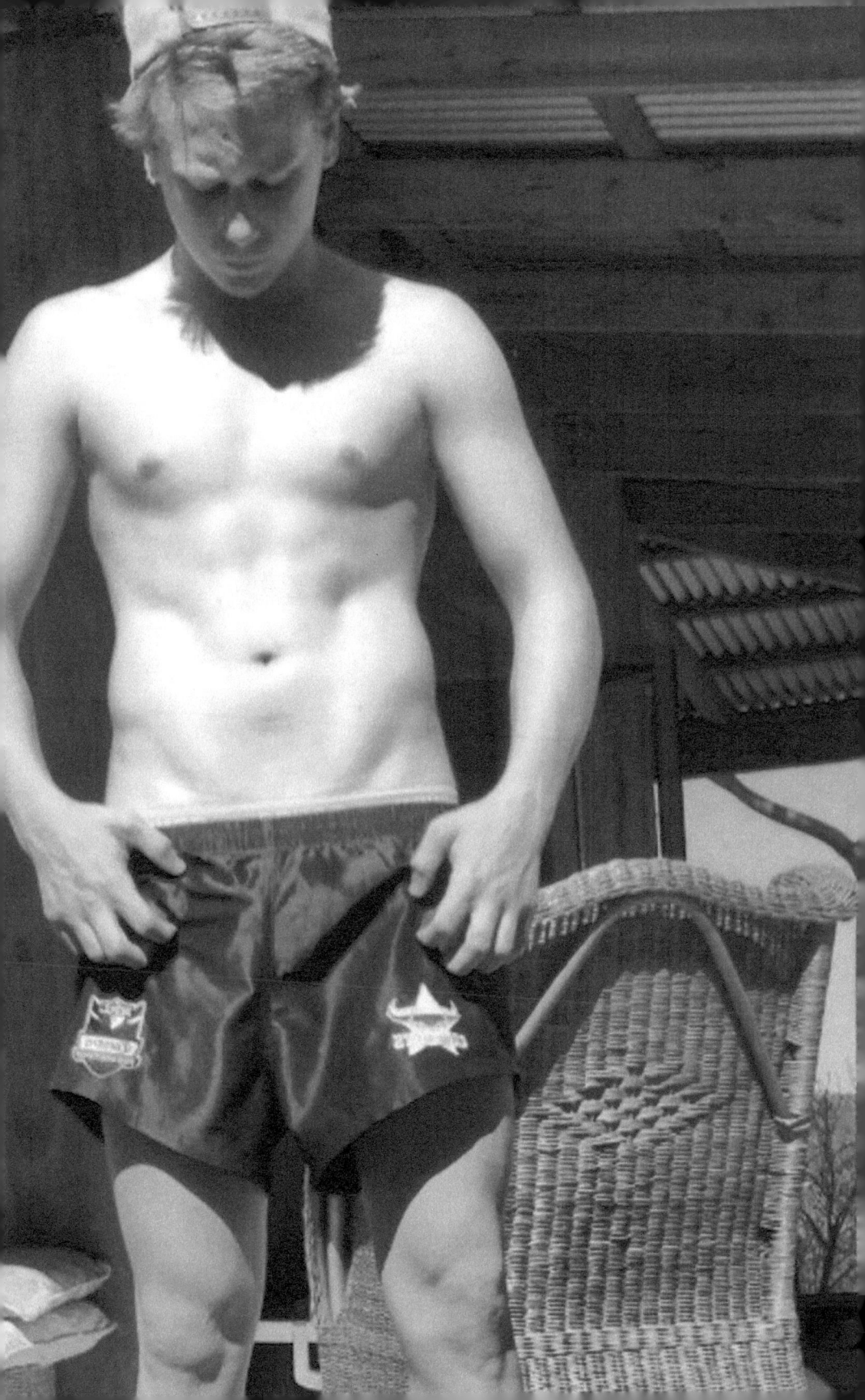

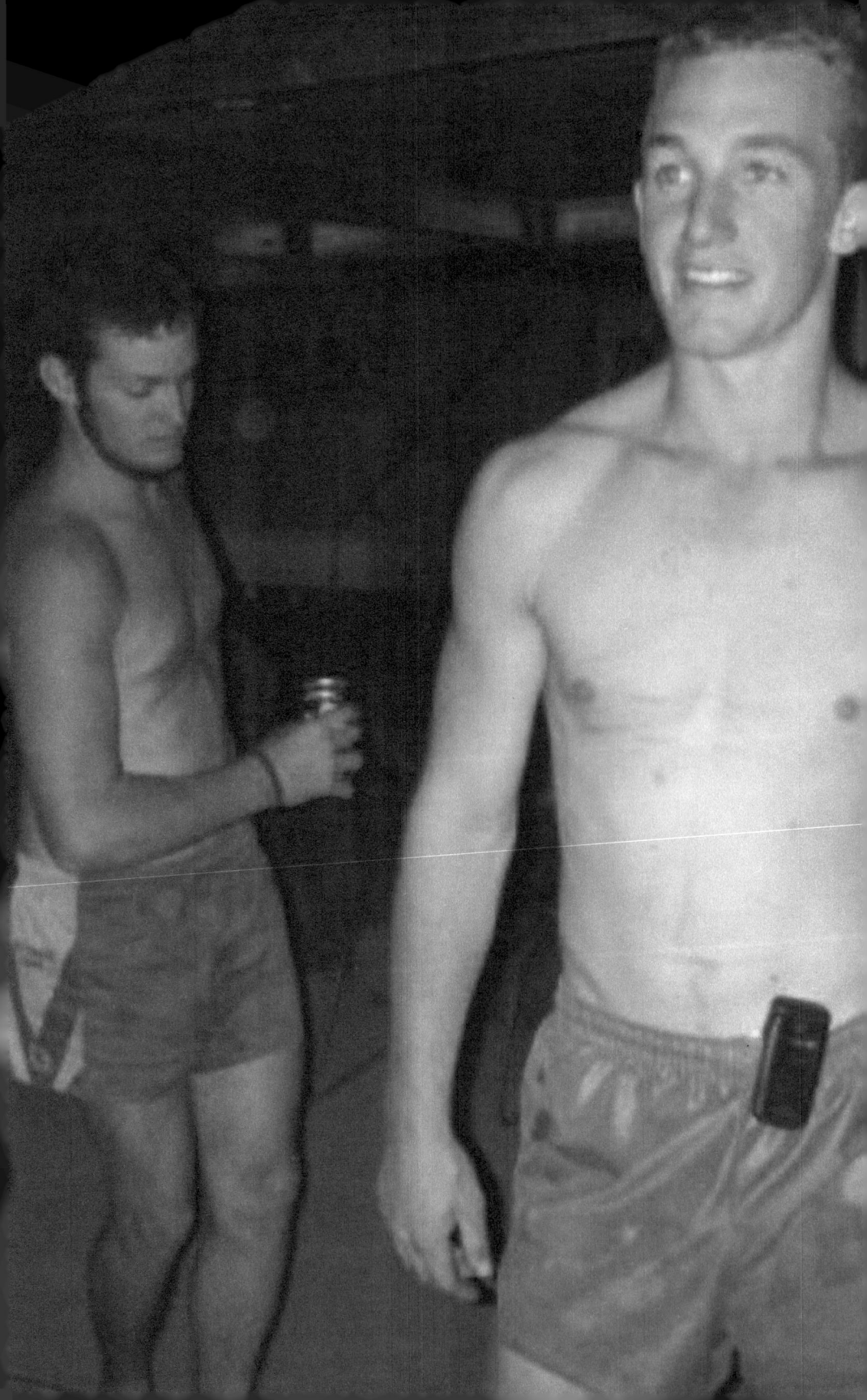

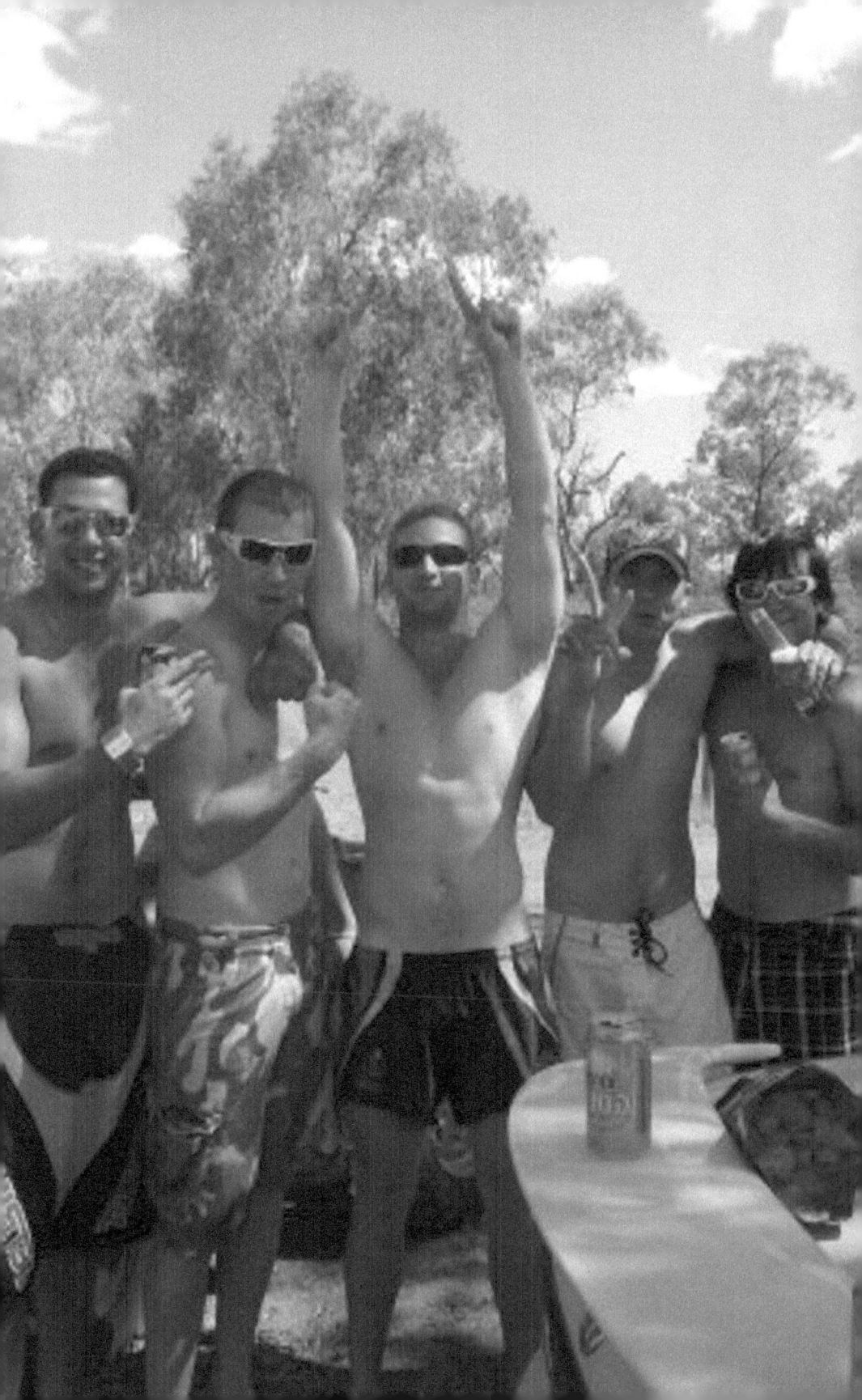

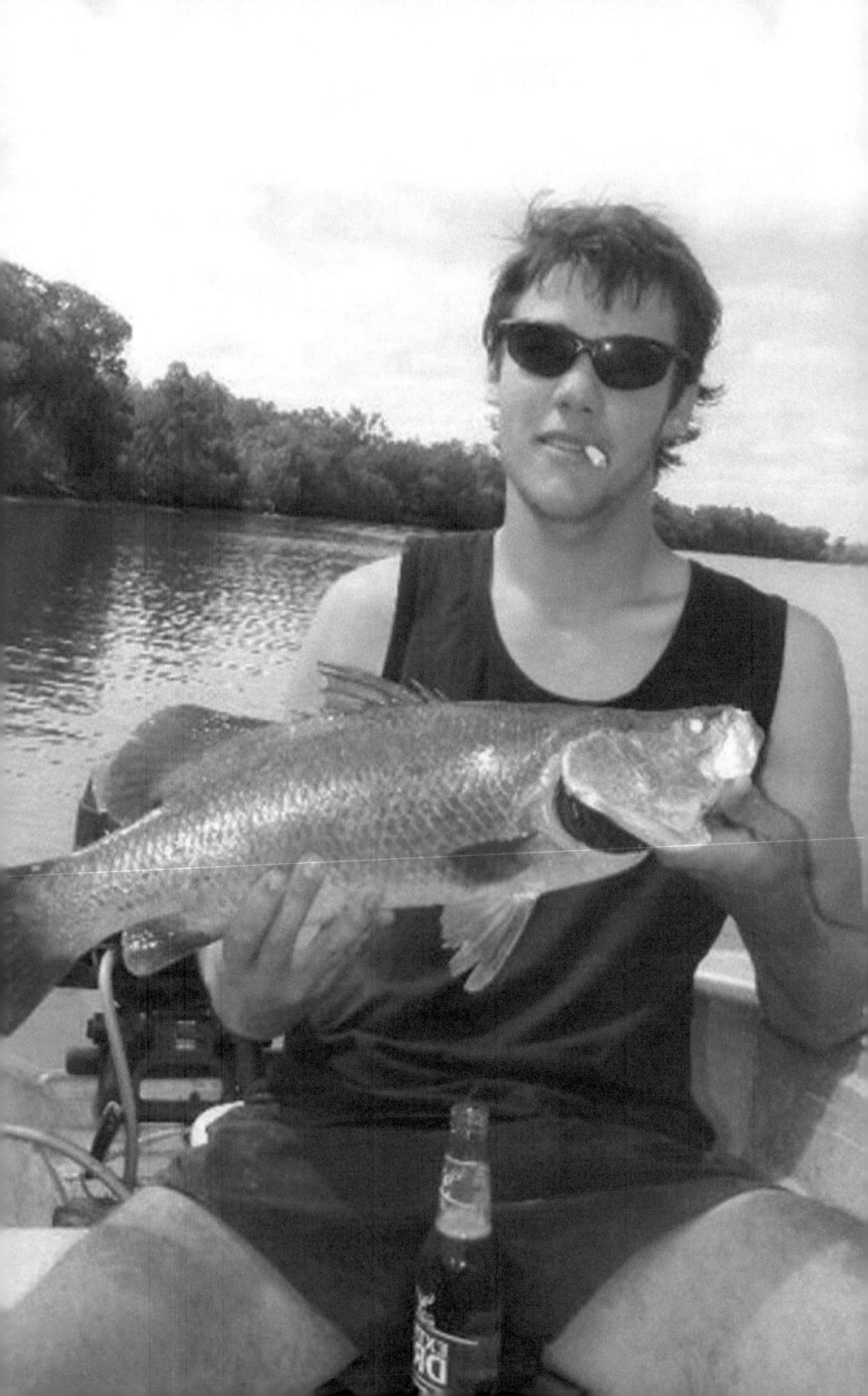

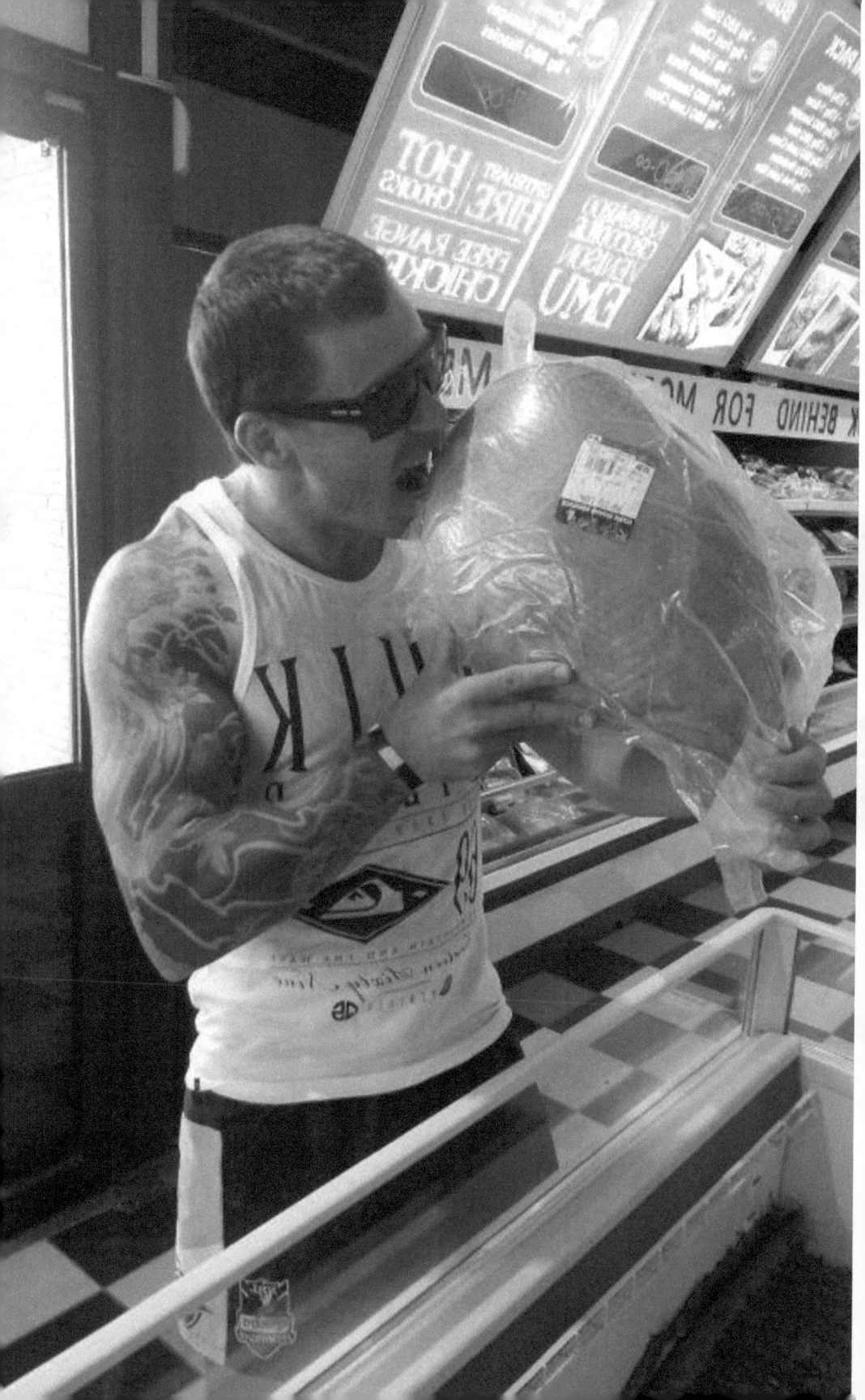

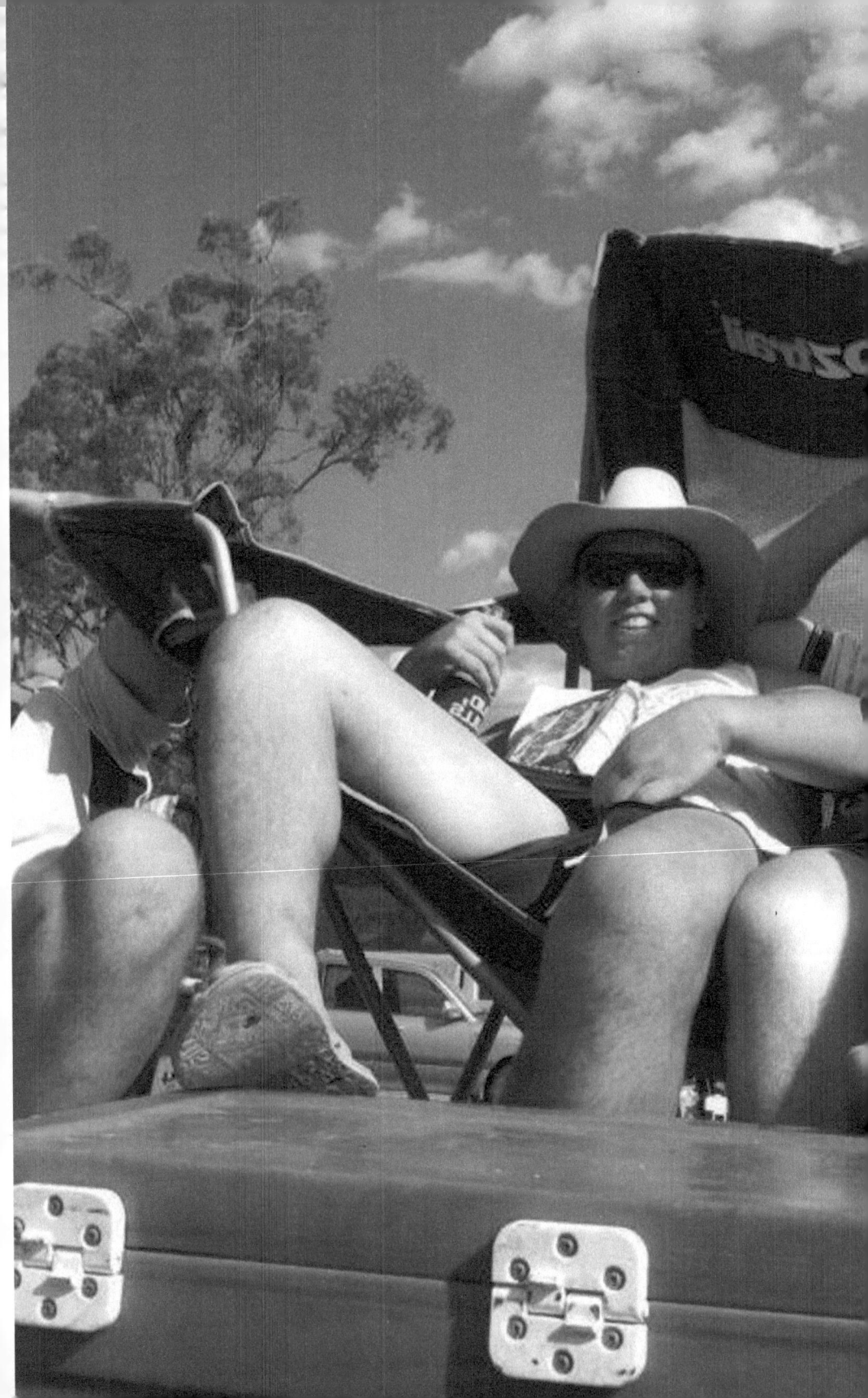

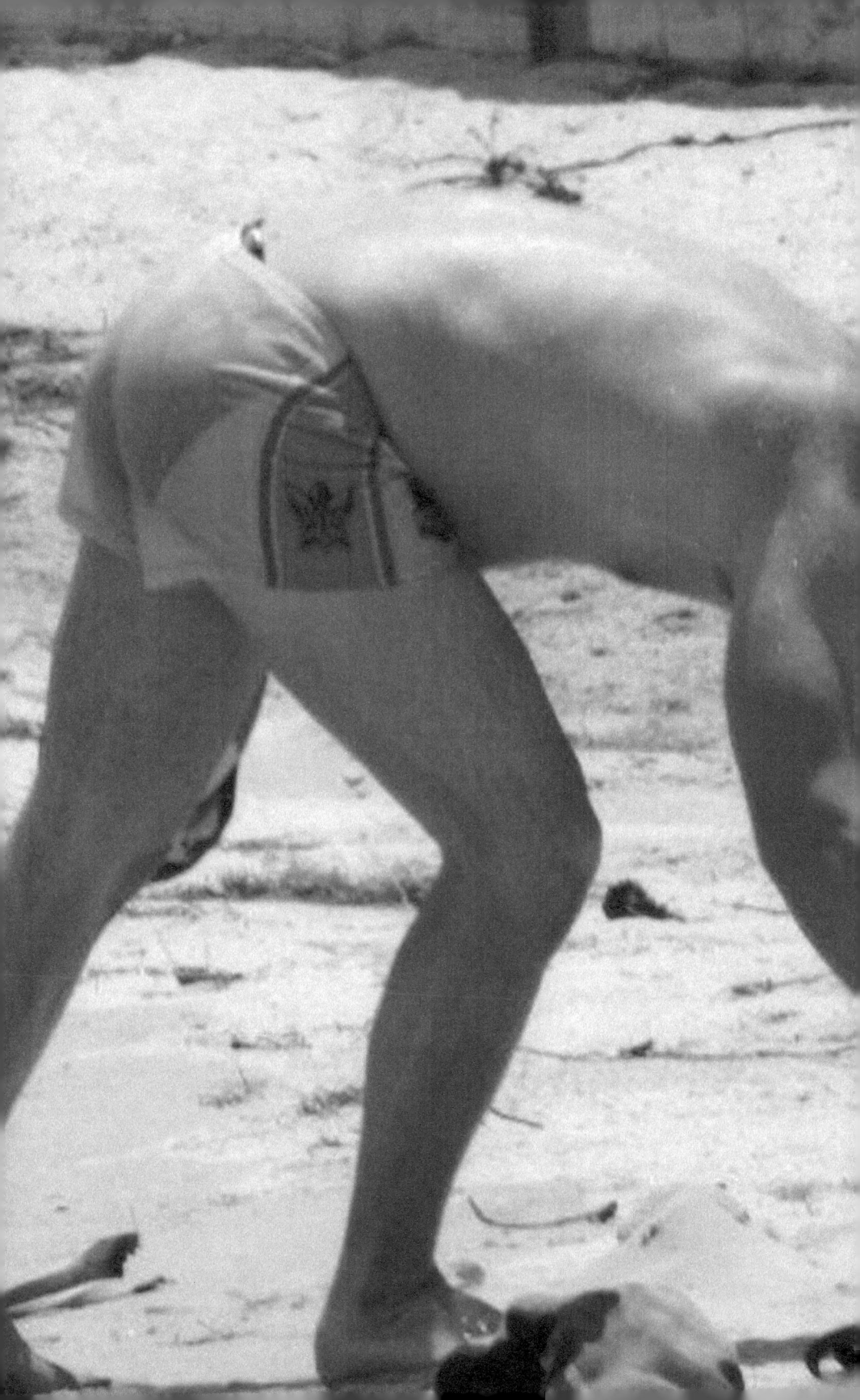

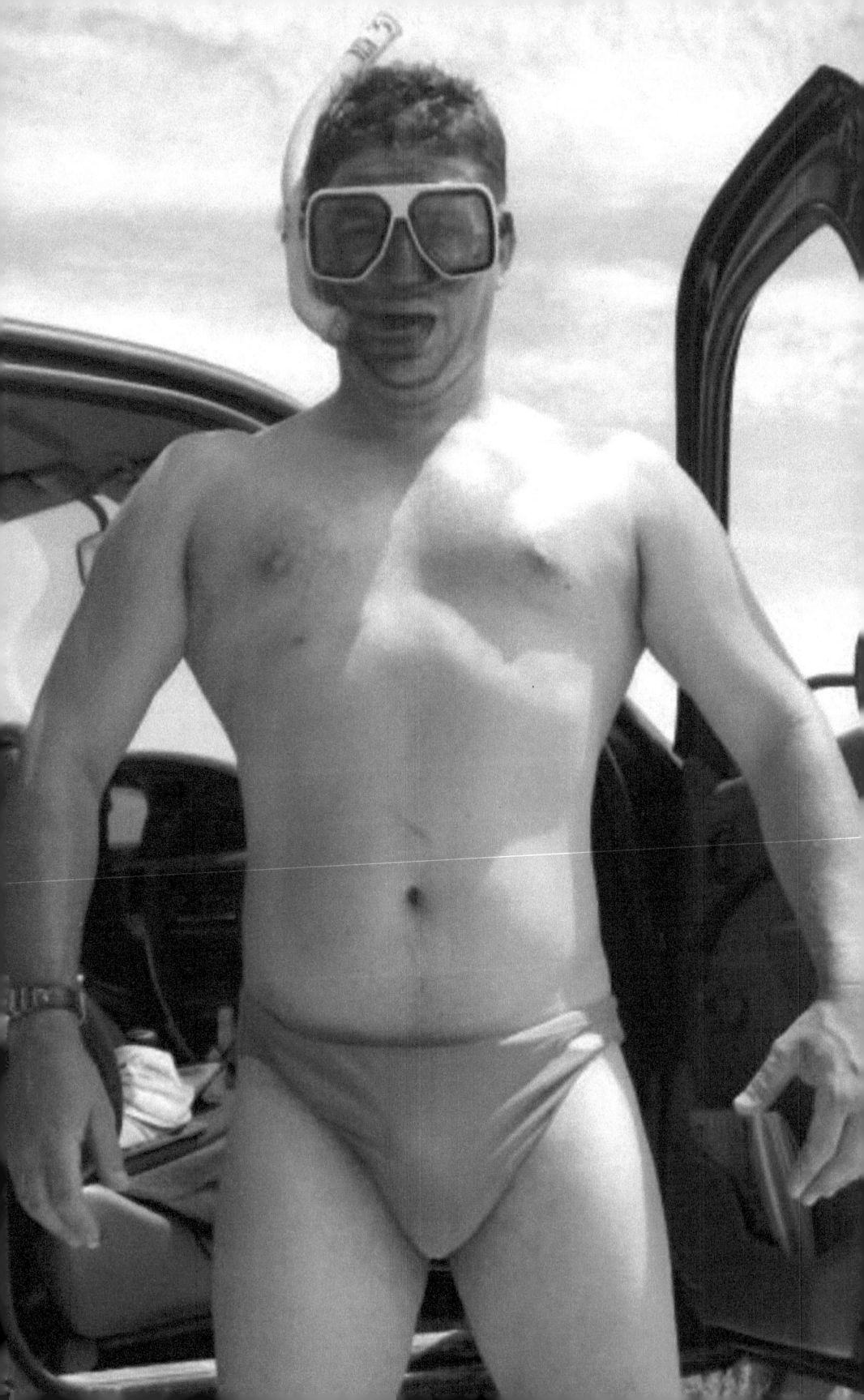

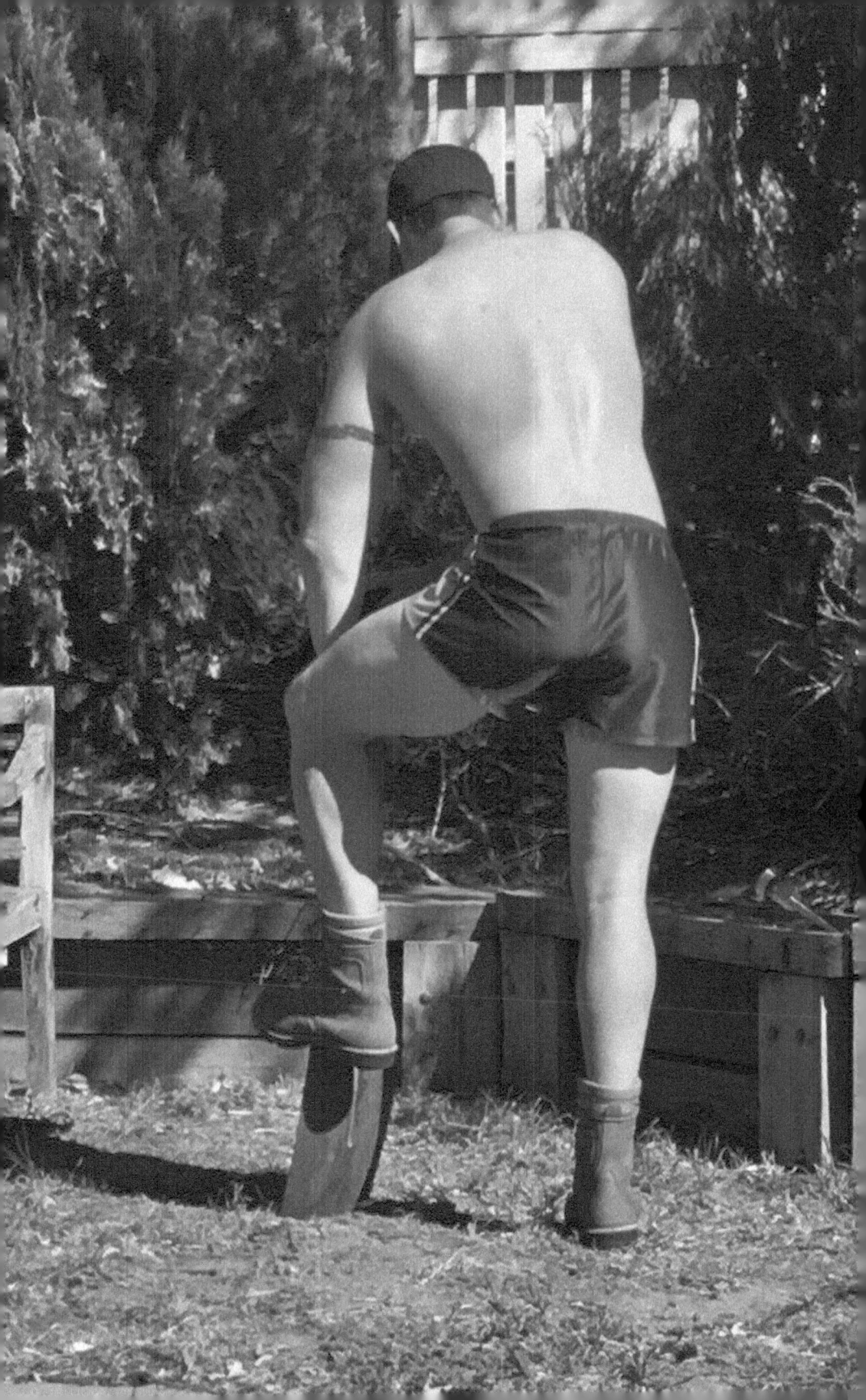

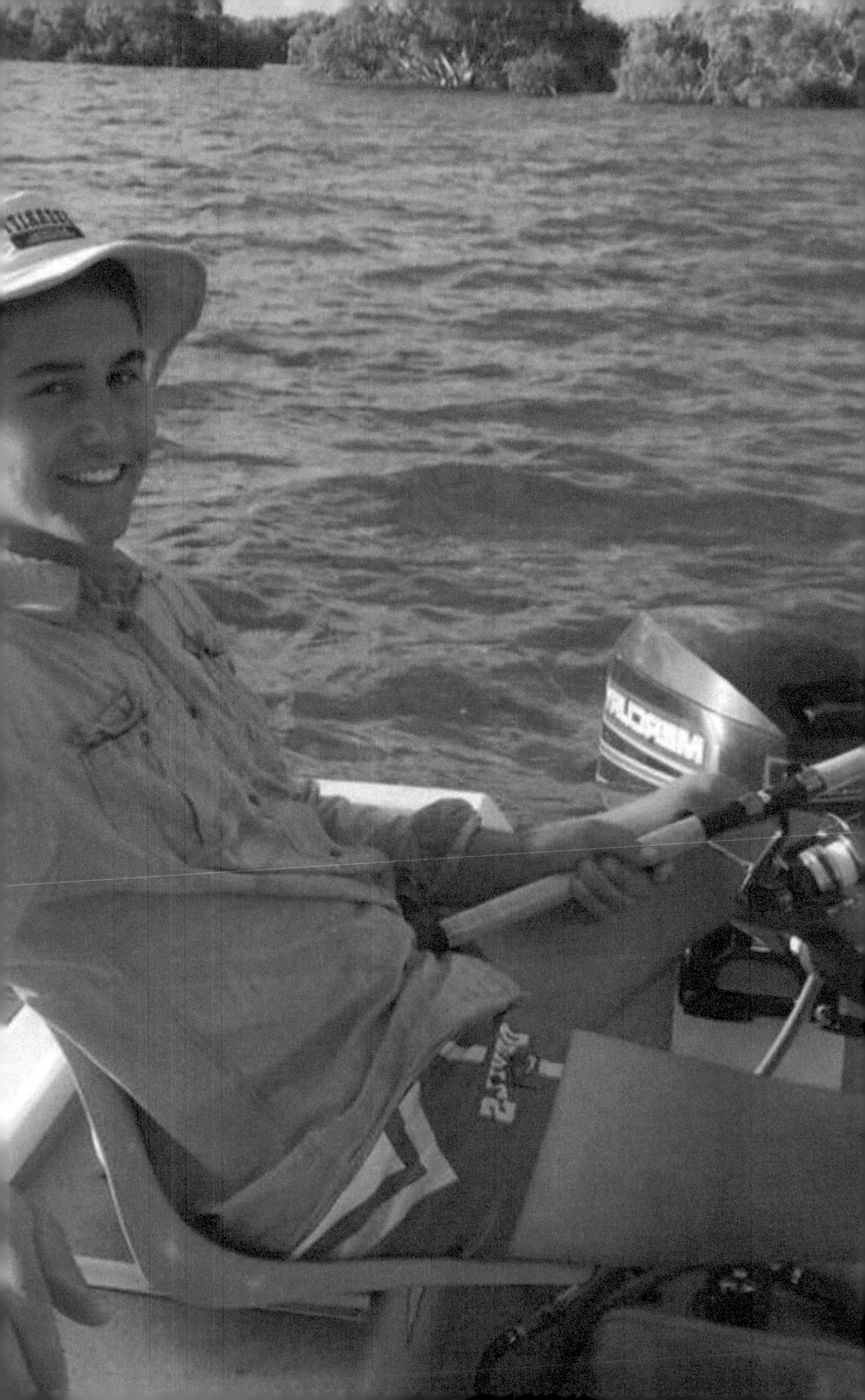

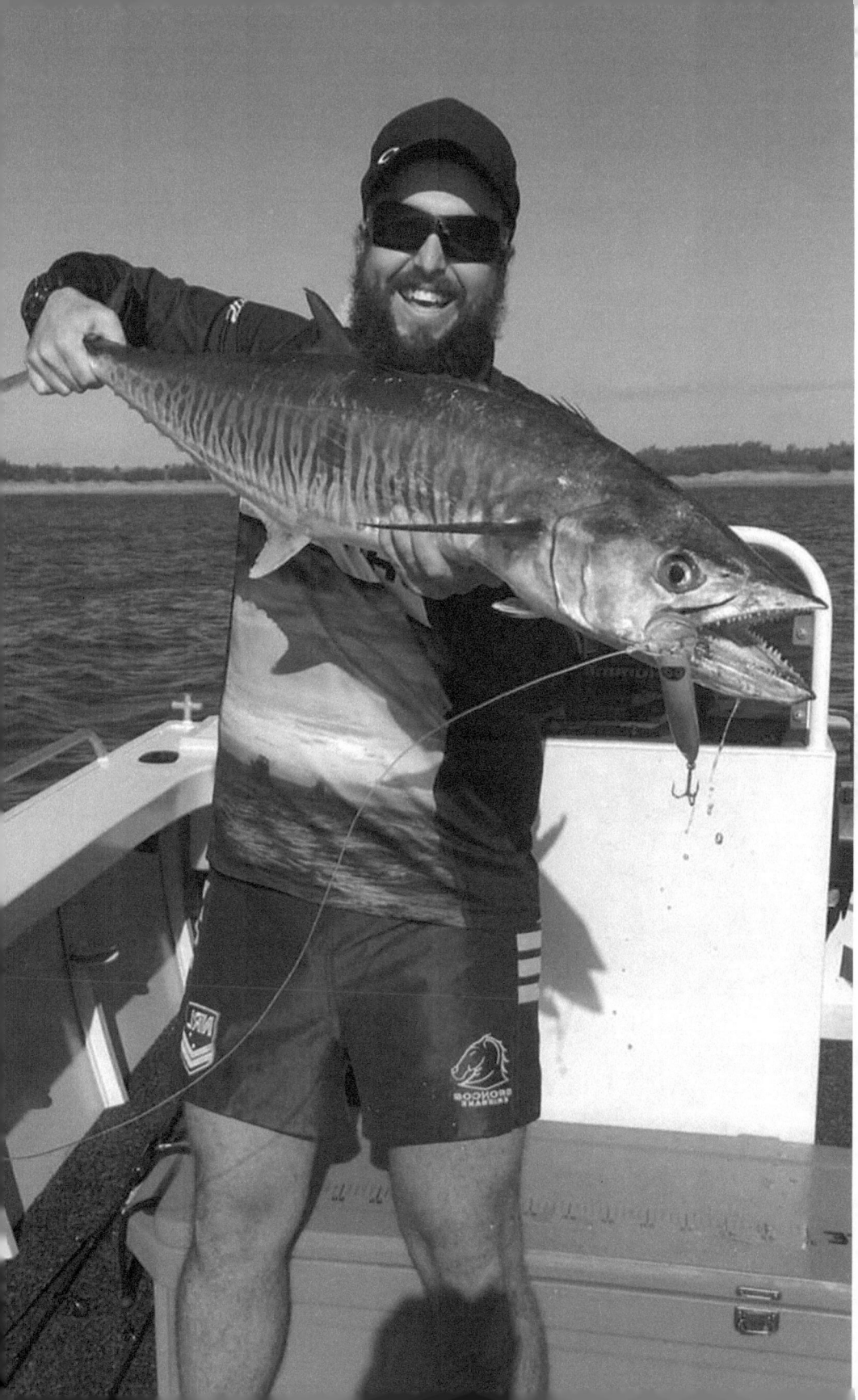

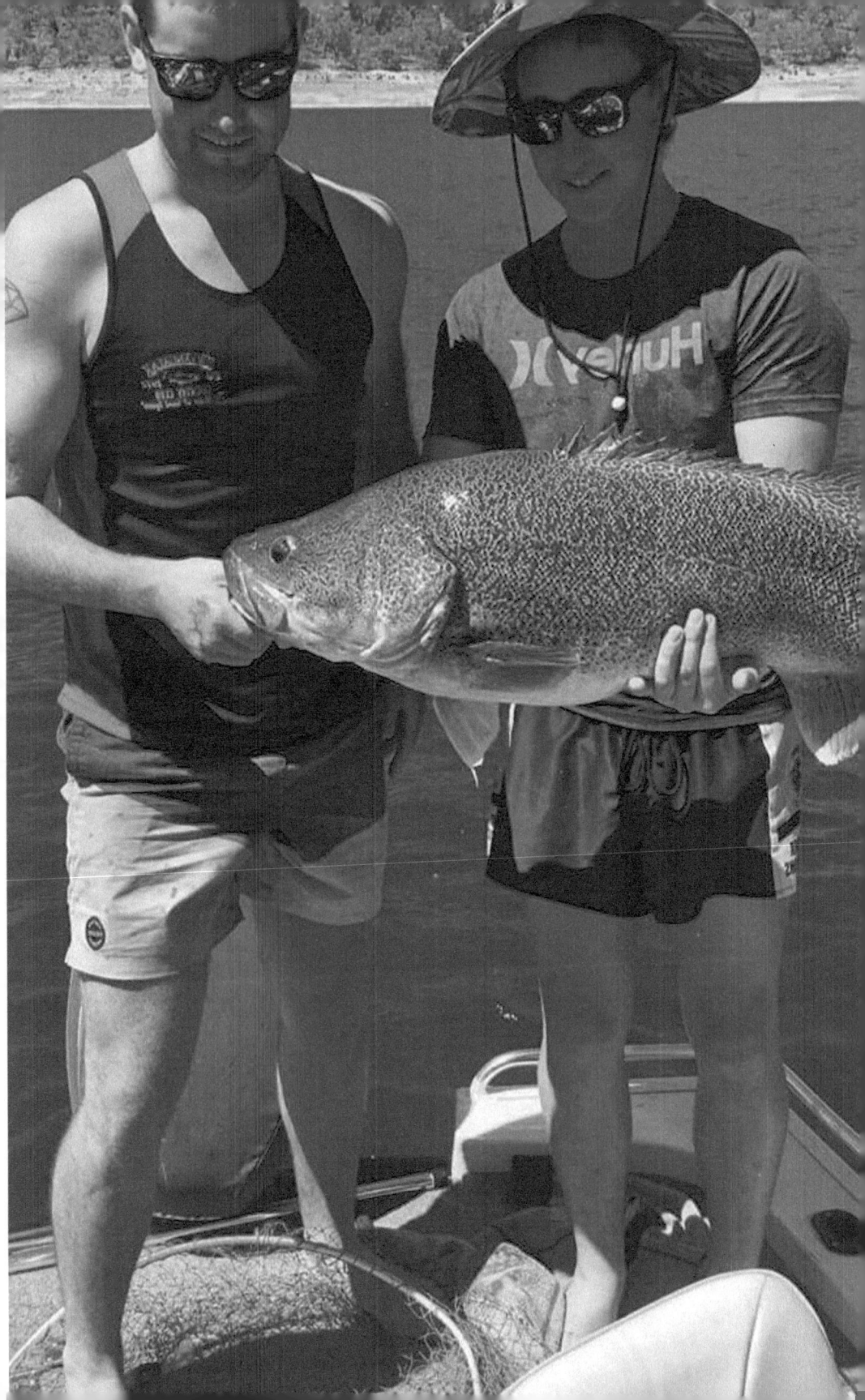

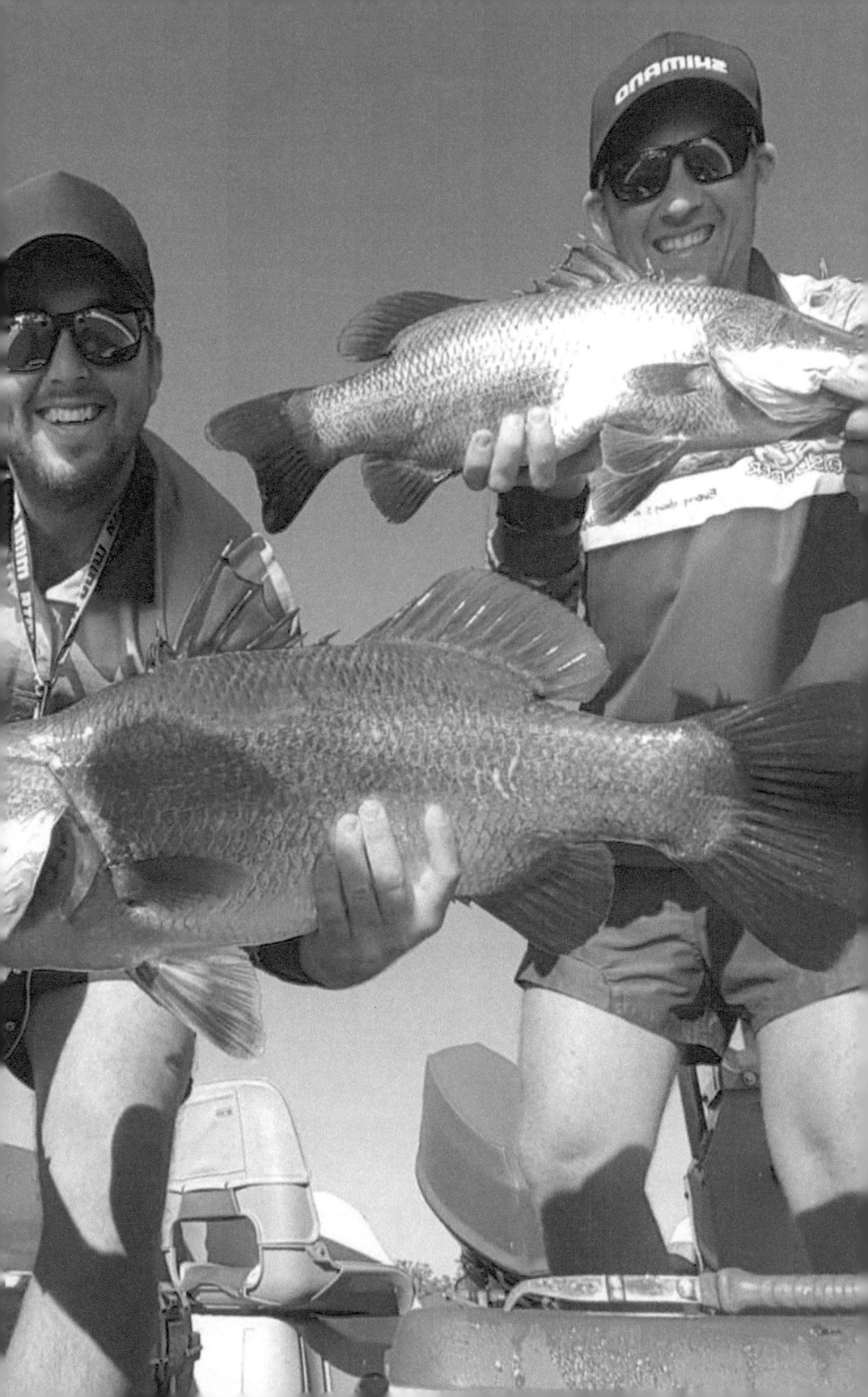

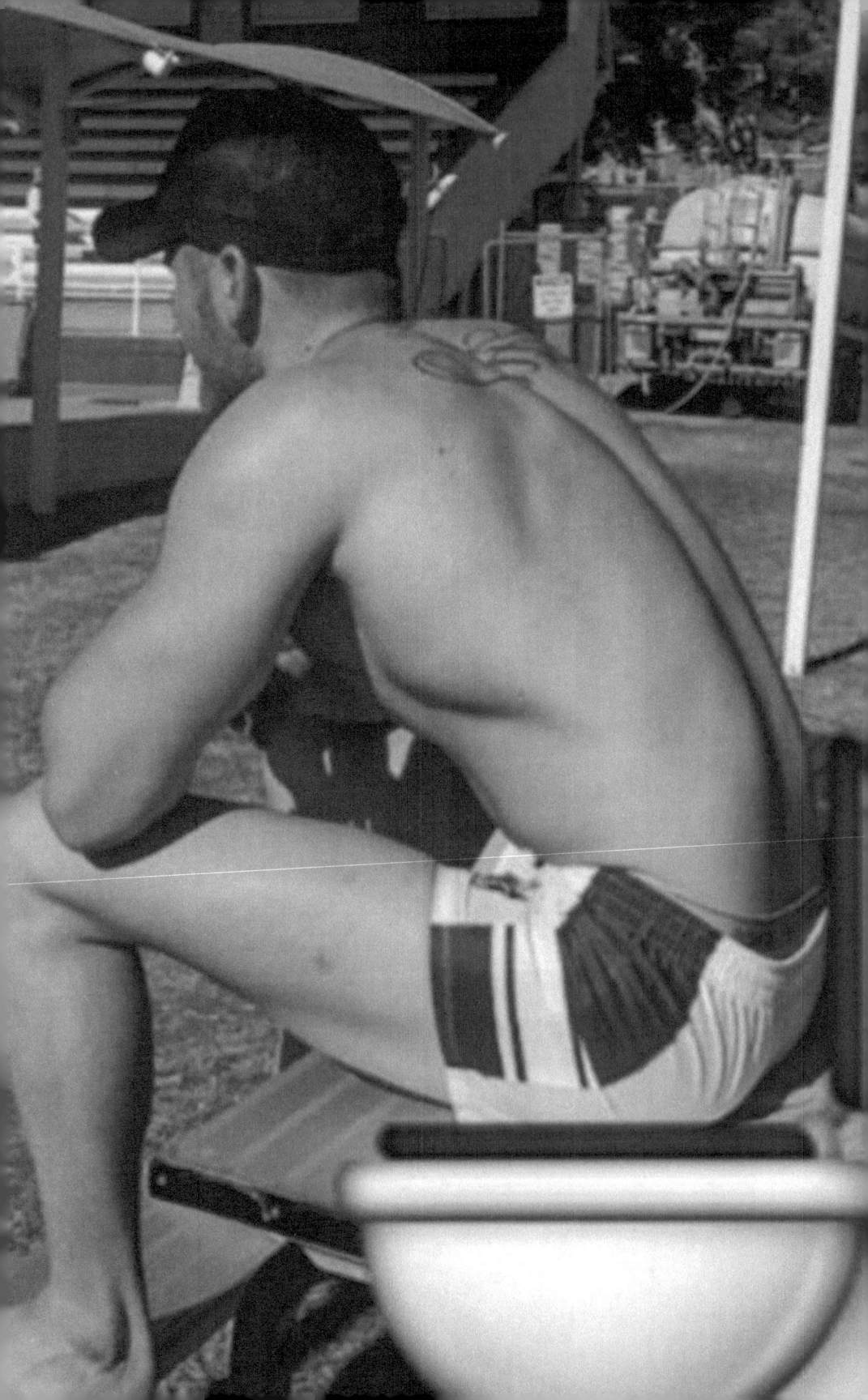

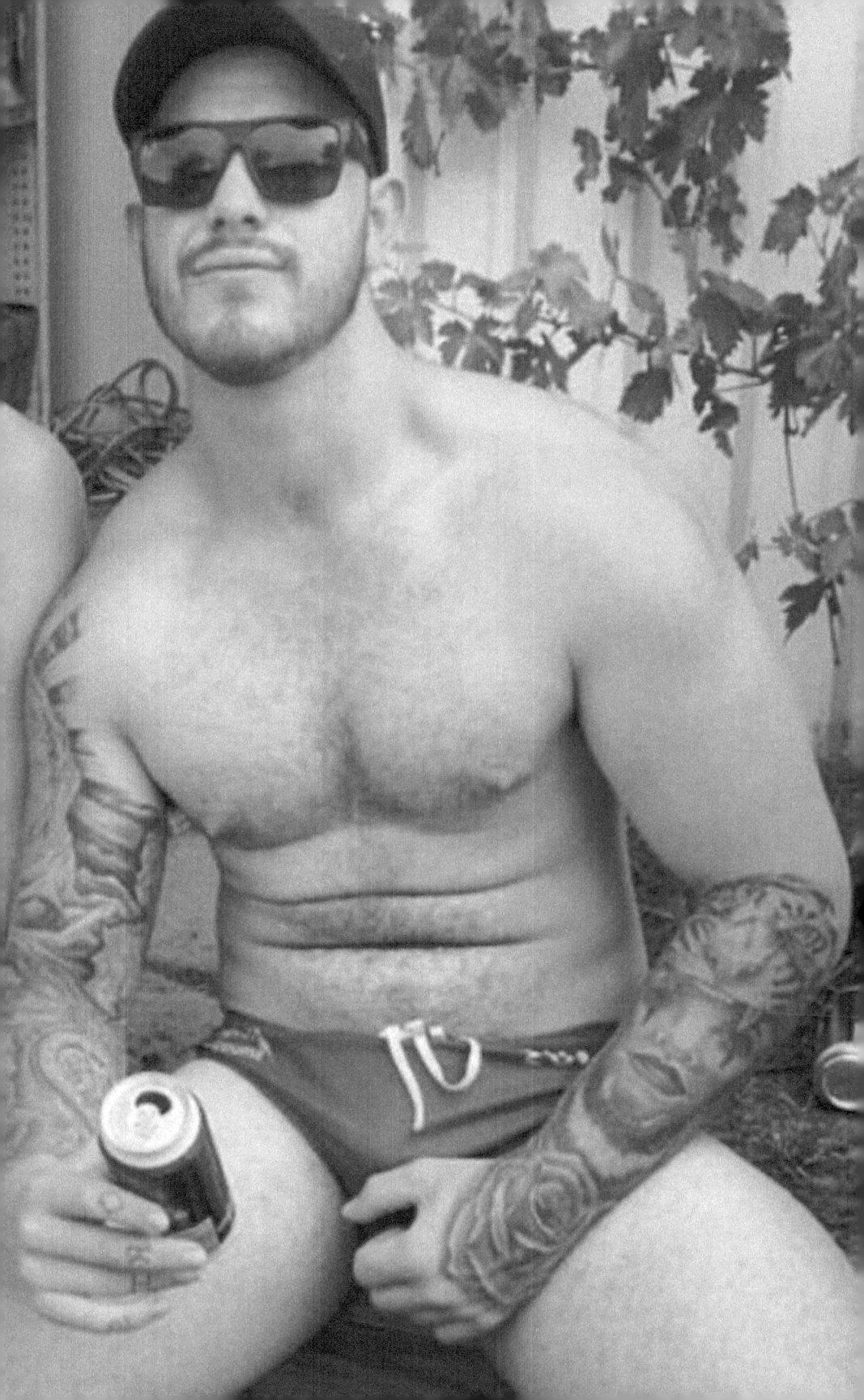

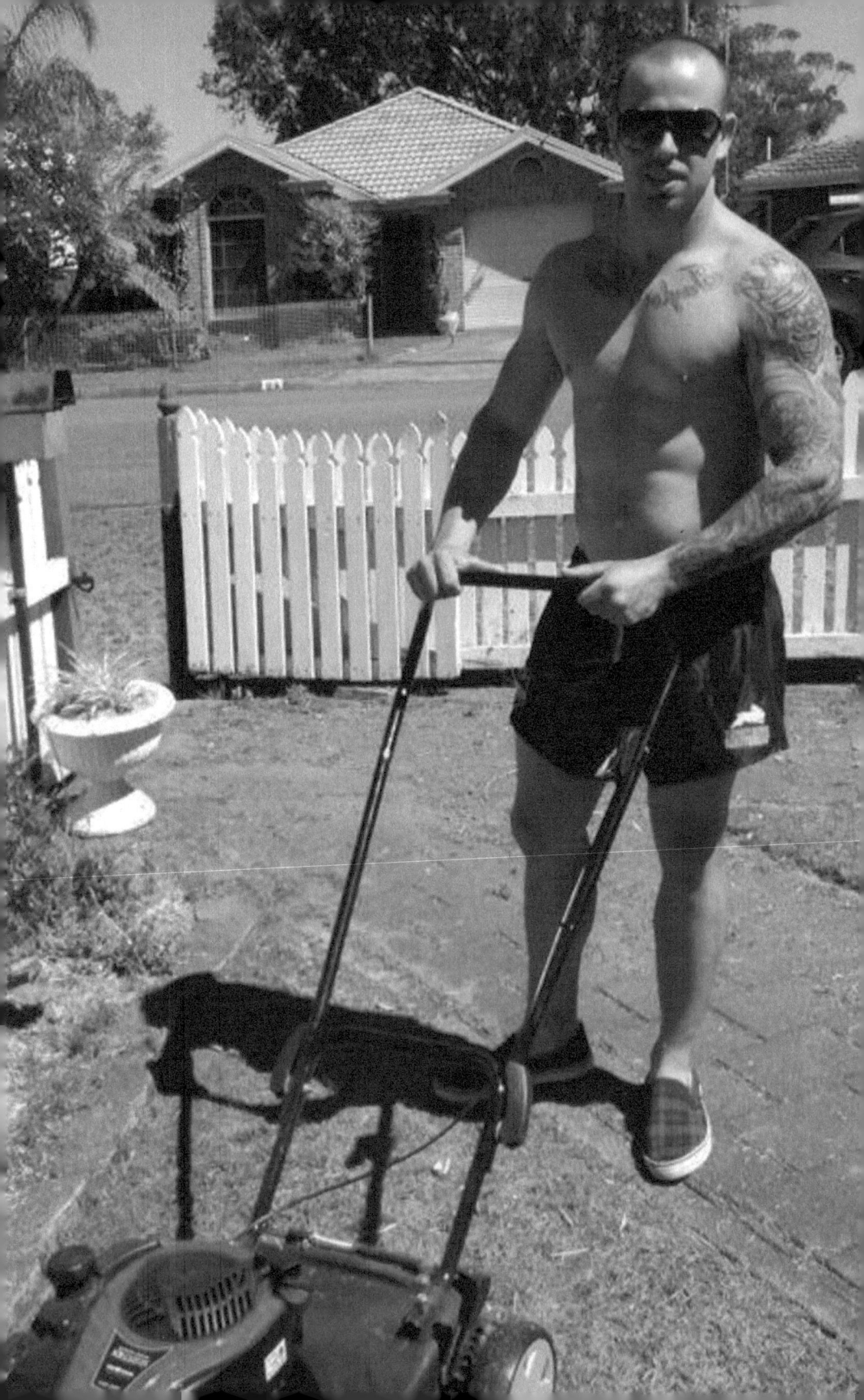

www.ingramcontent.com/pod-product-compliance
Lightning Source LLC
Chambersburg PA
CBHW021038180526
45163CB00005B/2176